ALADDIN'S- BOOKSHO

106, KING STREET,

RAMSGATE

INTR

by John A. Keel

60p

For twenty years a pathetic assortment of crackpots and cultists have ruled the "flying saucer field," screaming to an amused world that we are being invaded by tiny green men from some other planet, and passing on absurd messages of faith and good will which they claimed they received telepathically from the all-seeing, all-knowing "Brothers" in Outer Space. And for most of those twenty years the general press and the public have laughed at the "UFOnuts" and ridiculed anyone who reported seeing anything unusual in the sky.

The real mystery in this multi-faceted enigma, however, has been how our governments and our scientific establishment could overlook the astounding amount of sincere reports from honest, and often well-trained, citizens. Equally baffling, there has been an almost complete lack of reasonable, rational investigation into this subject. Hardcore "Ufologists," as they call themselves, have frantically collected random newspaper clippings and indulged in fanciful speculations based upon a narrow range of pseudo-scientific knowledge tainted with the mystical and the occult. Very few of the many books published on "flying saucers" have attempted to collate the available "hard facts" and review statistically the vast amount of data now available.

Now, at long last, a highly qualified science writer, Otto Binder, has reviewed this overwhelming mass of material—twenty years of sightings and information—and organized it into a meaningful and lucid book. He has done a remarkable job of sifting fact from fantasy and truth from nonsense. If there is a "secret" to the UFO mystery, it can be found somewhere in these pages.

While the fanatics and "contactees" of dubious character have been ranting about tall, blond Venusians who are coming to save us from the evils of our ways, thousands of more ordinary citizens have been living in the midst of a little publicized terror. They have been burned, paralyzed and, in a few cases, even killed by the presence of these mysterious objects in our skies. Brave Air Force pilots have died pursuing them. Our power systems, radios, and vehicles have been mysteriously blacked out or stalled when the UFO's were overhead. Thousands of witnesses have been harassed or ridiculed into silence, and official explanations for the phenomenon have steadily grown more absurd, hinting at some kind of governmental desperation. Mr. Binder skillfully gives us the whole story, with names, dates, and documentation. A story whose telling is long overdue.

The sacred cow of Science is reduced to hamburger in these pages, and our own pitiful inadequacies come sharply into focus when you consider the vastness of the Universe and the limitations of our knowledge. While we are spending billions to hurl slender firecrackers into space, our governments—and a large part of the public—still refuse to recognize the possibility that some life form somewhere else in space might be sending more sophisticated instruments to our own pathetic little mudball.

Those of us who have followed the UFO situation closely are beginning to realize that this is more than a "scientific problem." Much more. It encompasses the whole history of mankind and embraces all of the world's religions. A number of serious researchers now believe that the unidentified flying objects and their elusive occupants were here long before Man, himself, appeared, and that they will be here long after we have faded away. They may, in fact, be a natural part of our environment and may *never* enter into open contact with us.

Perhaps you, yourself, have seen something inexplicable in the sky. And you may have bought this book to find out something about what that "thing" was. It may comfort you to know that millions of others have also seen "flying saucers" and we do know much more about these things than most people realize. Here are all the facts and figures, along with the educated speculations of many experts. It all adds up to a hair-raising story—and may eventually prove to be the most important story in history. It has been ignored officially for years, but now as our lights dim, our cars stall, and our phones go dead, we cannot ignore it any longer. Somebody somewhere is trying to tell us something and it is time for us to listen.

—JOHN A. KEEL
New York
June 29, 1967

What We Really Know About FLYING SAUCERS

Otto Binder

A FAWCETT GOLD MEDAL BOOK

Fawcett Publications, Inc., Greenwich, Conn.

Member of American Book Publishers Council, Inc.

To
MARY LORINE BINDER
my beloved daughter

(deceased March 27, 1967)

CONDITIONS OF SALE: This book is sold subject to the condition that it shall not, by way of trade or otherwise, be lent, resold, hired out or otherwise circulated without the publisher's prior consent, and without a similar condition including this condition being imposed on the subsequent purchaser.

Copyright © 1967 by Fawcett Publications, Inc.

All rights reserved, including the right to reproduce this book or any portions thereof.

Printed in the United States of America

Contents

ACKNOWLEDGMENTS

The author wishes to express gratitude for the aid he received and data utilized, from such UFOlogists as James Moseley (*Saucer News*), Gene Duplantier (*Science, Space & Saucers*), Robert Gribble (*NICAP Reporter/Seattle*), *Ray Palmer* (*Flying Saucers & Search*), Joan and Jean of *Saucer Scoop*, and such UFO experts as Tim Beckley, George D. Fawcett, Brayce Gembler, and others who would make this list too long. Also the authors of various saucer books, particularly Dr. Jacques Vallee and Aime Michel, and Major Donald Keyhoe, to whom I owe an extra thanks for permission to use data, sightings, and charts from *The UFO Evidence*, NICAP's masterful UFO roundup. My appreciation also to Mr. Richard Hall. Finally, thanks must go to U. F. O. I. R. C. and its invaluable compilation, *The Reference for Outstanding UFO Sighting Reports* (published by the UFO Information Retrieval Service, Inc., Riderwood, Maryland) from which I excerpted liberally. This is not to imply that the above have in any way endorsed or passed upon the contents of this book, and its opinions or conclusions, which are purely my own.

The photographs on pages 49, 50, 51, 63, 99, 101, 109, 128, 131, 134, 146, 162, 175, 176 are from the collection of August C. Roberts.

CHAPTER 1

UFO Patterns: Prelude to Proof?

ALL WAS NORMAL in the everyday world as Waldo J. Harris, a real-estate broker, sat in his private plane at 3:14 P.M. on October 2, 1961, waiting his turn to take off from the airport at Salt Lake City, Utah.

At 3:15 the abnormal came along when he noticed a bright spot in the southern sky. He had to concentrate on his takeoff then as the control tower gave him clearance. While trimming his climb-out he again glanced south and was surprised to see the object in about the same position.

Airborne and about to turn downwind, he was still more startled to see the peculiar light still hovering in that same place. Now gnawingly curious and free of the traffic pattern, he turned to get a closer look at whatever amazing thing was hanging so mysteriously in the sky.

"As I drew nearer," he reported later to NICAP (National Investigations Committee on Aerial Phenomena), "I could see that the object had no wings nor tail nor any other exterior control surfaces protruding from what appeared to be the fuselage. It seemed to be hovering with a little rocking motion."

Now it began moving for the first time and "as it rocked away from me I could see that it was a disc-shaped object. I would guess its diameter at about fifty to fifty-five feet, the thickness at the middle about eight to ten feet. It had the appearance of sand-blasted aluminum."

From the unusual it now became the fantastic.

"It rose abruptly about one thousand feet above me as I closed in." After the UFO flew some 10 miles away, Mr. Harris reported: "I again approached the object but not so closely this time, when it . . . went completely out of sight in two or three seconds. As you know, I can keep our fastest jets in sight for several minutes, so you can see that this object was moving rather rapidly."

A classic understatement, as it must have been streaking away at upward of 5,000 mph.

What should we think of this incredible report? Was Mr. Harris seeing some sort of private illusion? No, because 8 or 10 people on the ground at the Utah airport, who were interviewed by NICAP, also saw the object perform the same maneuvers at the same time.

Could it have been some conventional object seen under deceptive conditions?

—*Balloon?* Obviously eliminated; wrong shape.

—*Star or planet?* Not in the daytime.

—*Bird or bird flock?* Too sharply defined.

—*Experimental USAF craft?* Secret new designs are hardly tested near busy airports with many eyes—and spies—within range.

—*Experimental Soviet craft?* They would certainly not be making a test flight within easy reach of the USAF.

—*Mirage?* Eight or ten witnesses, at different points around the airport, could not possibly see the same mirage as the man in the plane, since such illusions depend on the observer's fixed position.

—*Atmosphere inversion* (false aerial image)? No inversion was reported in that vicinity for that date by the Weather Bureau.

—*Hallucination?* Then 8 or 10 other people, none knowing the other or comparing notes, had the same hallucination at the same time—which is medically impossible.

We have gone through the list of possibilities, just as the Air Force does with each UFO sighting. And like the Air Force's conclusion, our only conclusion can be—UNIDENTIFIED, UNKNOWN OBJECT.

Definitions

Before we go any further, we will assume that many readers are unfamiliar with flying saucer books or the intricacies of the UFO field of investigation as carried on by the Air Force and by private groups. A few definitions and clarifications are then necessary.

What is a UFO? "UFO," *Unidentified Flying Object,* is the term given by the U.S. Air Force to the more popularly known "flying saucers." Some sectors of the USAF prefer the term UAO—Unidentified Aerial Object—since the word *flying* implies a machine, and the Air Force believes that to be an unproved assumption.

A *known* is the USAF's vernacular for a UFO that has been explained as some natural phenomenon. More rarely it is then called an IFO, for Identified Flying Object.

An *unknown* is a UFO that has never been satisfactorily explained, or explained away. *This is the true UFO.*

Are "flying saucers" the same as UFO's? Yes, Flying saucers was the popular term invented by the press in 1947 when Kenneth Arnold reported his famous sighting of nine "saucerlike" objects near Mount Rainier. Originally it meant only the disc-shaped or saucerlike form but has since come to cover any and all UFO's of any conceivable shape—namely, anything that moves, hovers, or maneuvers in the sky and is a nonconventional or unknown object.

Was Kenneth Arnold's sighting the first one? No, although it was the key, and kicked off the flying saucer controversy in America. UFO's were reported as early as 1946 in Europe, with Sweden's eerie "ghost rockets." In fact, reports very similar to flying saucer sightings have been recorded for centuries, so that it does not seem to be a peculiar phenomenon of the 20th century. It has simply come into prominence in our time.

Has America had the most UFO sightings? No more *on the average* than any other part of the world. This fact is not generally known to American citizens because both the government's policy of denying the "mystery" and the laxity of the press in covering foreign UFO reports have combined to give the false impression that flying saucers have chosen the U. S. as their favorite haunting grounds.

What are the UFO "waves"? Time and again, sightings have suddenly increased in various localities around the earth—America in 1952, France in 1954, South America in 1957, etc. During a wave over any certain region, sightings jump to fantastically high figures, sometimes 50 or 100 per day. Then, after a few weeks or months, they as mysteriously subside.

A new wave then starts somewhere else on earth or may already be in progress before the other wave has halted. In at least one case, the summer of 1954, there was a worldwide wave in which every area of earth reported a high incidence of UFO sightings.

Are the UFO's a proven fact? Hardly. It is, at present, purely a *supposition* based on circumstantial evidence that strange flying machines account for the unknowns— a viewpoint that the Air Force, our government, and many scientists steadfastly deny.

What is Project Blue Book? This is the official project of the USAF for investigating UFO's. Preceding it were Project Sign (January 1948 to February 1949) and Project Grudge (February 1949 to September 1951).

From 1951 to date, Project Blue Book has handled all UFO reports through the ATIC (Air Technical Intelligence Center) at Wright-Patterson AFB, Ohio. To date, Project Blue Book has processed more than 11,000 sightings, declaring only 652 to be unknowns.

But private "UFOlogy" groups contend that the USAF "recognizes" only a low percentage of sightings (less than one-tenth of the total) and that by statistical juggling it has hidden the fact that its true unknowns are 20 to 30 percent of the totals.

Through certain directives from Air Force headquarters Project Blue Book has muffled all sightings by its own pilots in the past few years and has also intimidated commercial airline pilots from reporting theirs (as stated in the various books of Major Donald E. Keyhoe and reaffirmed by NICAP).

Are the UFO's illusions? No. Far too many authenticated sightings of solid objects have been reported from reliable witnesses all over the world for the saucers to be any form of mass hallucination or self-delusion.

There has, in fact, been a subtle but definite change in

the official attitude toward UFO's recently to where few if any authorities will categorically state that flying saucers are unreal (illusionary) phenomena.

In short, it is now generally accepted that people do see something *real* in the sky in the case of the genuine unknowns. Just *what* those real things are remains the undecided question.

Can the UFO's be natural phenomena? Possibly but not probably, according to "UFOlogists." It is untenable to suppose that some kind of undiscovered aerial objects —say new forms of ball lightning, for instance—can account for the innumerable sightings of what seem to be metallic craft. The gap is too great to be bridged by so easy an explanation. Nor can marsh gas, ionized air, or any such atmospheric conditions duplicate the appearance and maneuverings of UFO's.

What is a temperature inversion? Sometimes a layer of warm air will rest over a layer of cold air, with a high temperature differential from 9° to 18°. Under these very special and uncommon conditions the surface where they meet acts as a mirror or distorting lens, casting false images from the sky or the ground in front of the observer's eye. It is true that inversions cause a certain small percentage of false UFO sightings but not nearly so often as some authorities imply. It has never explained away the many "classic" cases of true unknowns.

Who is Dr. J. Allen Hynek? Dr. Hynek, chairman of the astronomy department of Northwestern University, has for some 20 years been the Air Force's civilian "expert" on UFO's. He was called in for all major sightings and through the years he has explained many of them as natural objects—planes, birds, planets, balloons—mistaken for UFO's. However, he has within the recent past publicly stated that he believes the mystery is unsolved and that "science can no longer ignore the UFO phenomenon."

Are UFO's being investigated scientifically? Yes, since November of 1966, in America. Under an Air Force grant of $310,000 Dr. Edward U. Condon of the University of Colorado has organized a team of scientists who are checking all USAF flying saucer reports and all other aspects of the UFO riddle. Some say that this will be a "whitewash" of the USAF's policy of denigrating saucers.

What is the "invisible college"? The "invisible college" is a worldwide group of renowned scientists—astronomers, astrophysicists, chemists, biologists, anthropologists, etc.—who have secretly agreed to investigate UFO's on their own, entirely independently of the Air Force, the Condon Committee, or any government. They are exchanging data and sightings and striving to come to some definitive conclusion about the UFO's, without any preconceived judgments in advance.

Many members of this "UFO underground" are at present anonymous in that their reputations might be injured if it were known that they gave any credence whatsoever to flying saucers. But they are determined to prove that "orthodox" science is wrong in ignoring the UFO phenomenon. They hope to be able to come out in the open someday without stigma and also to organize an international UFO investigative body within the UN or separately.

What are "UFOlogists"? Under this self-invented name various civilians have grouped together, starting as early as 1952, to investigate flying saucers on their own, deploring the fact that the scientific community chose to ignore this amazing worldwide phenomenon.

In the main, the UFOlogists are sober, sensible American citizens who have no axe to grind and are simply avidly curious about the UFO's. Contrary to public opinion, the lunatic fringe and crackpot element are only a small portion of these serious "students" of UFOlogy.

What are the "contactees"? The so-called contactees are various people who claim to have contacted the flying saucer folk, to have even ridden in their vehicles, and in some cases to have visited their home worlds. Their stories of course are highly questionable, and not the slightest valid proof has ever been offered to back up their sensational claims.

Be it noted that this book, without any implications, will not examine or include any contactee claims at all, dealing only with bona fide sightings by reliable witnesses.

This has to be made clear. Too many scientists and average citizens have tended to sneer and scoff at the UFO's simply because a certain element of irresponsible people has "hitched its wagon to flying stars." We trust that the reader will not therefore condemn UFOlogy—the legitimate and earnest study of the UFO phenomenon—because of those loud, brash, publicity-seeking non-UFOlogists in the contactee class.

What is NICAP? NICAP stands for the National Investigations Committee on Aerial Phenomena, organized in 1956 by Major Donald E. Keyhoe, ex-Marine. It is representative of the many other private groups of UFOlogists and is the most prestigious. NICAP's openly avowed belief is that the flying saucers are interstellar craft from other worlds in outer space.

NICAP has published a monumental book, *The UFO Evidence,* which analyzes some 746 sightings in detail, all of them bona fide unknowns. They freely admit they have not yet proven their case, and their perennial demand is for a Congressional investigation and/or official government acknowledgment that the UFO mystery must be treated seriously and studied scientifically. They have seemingly won one point in the formation of the Condon Committee—if it is not an Air Force whitewash attempt.

This book quotes liberally from *The UFO Evidence* for its invaluable data and documented sightings. Those interested in joining this organization may send the dues ($5 per year) to—

> MEMBERSHIP DEPT.
> NICAP
> 1536 CONNECTICUT AVE., N.W.
> WASHINGTON, D.C. 20036

Categories

To return to Waldo J. Harris, his sighting is "typical" for several reasons. It involves a *disc*-shaped object that looked *metallic* and hovered with a *rocking* motion, then shot away at unbelievable *speed*. There are literally hundreds of this particular kind of sighting, for the UFO's are not a haphazard series of unrelated and unique objects.

On the contrary, they fall into definite *patterns*.

Analyses and breakdowns of over 11,000 Air Force reports in the past 20 years, plus at least an equal number of well-documented sightings gathered by NICAP and other UFOlogy organizations, have now brought forth the rough outlines of a way to systematically group the UFO's into distinct categories.

NICAP has already begun to do this with sample listings of selected cases and has charted a series of distinct shapes of UFO's—discs, spheroids, ovoids, stars, footballs, teardrops, and "cigars." These types, with variations, repeat over and over. There is little question that in many cases, especially with the ubiquitous "discs," millions of people in America and around the world have reported the *same type* of unknown.

Yes, *millions!* A Gallup Poll in 1966 revealed that 5 million Americans believe they have seen UFO's, through a period of 20 years. Since America has one-tenth the world's population, and since saucers are reported from every area on earth, a staggering total of 50 million humans presumably have seen UFO's since 1947.

Of these perhaps 80% are false sightings by befuddled or unreliable witnesses who saw only stars, balloons, birds, and what have you. The remaining 20%, or 10,-000,000 sightings in 20 years, can be assumed to be genuine, or some 500,000 worldwide sightings per year.

Out of these, taking the NICAP percentage, 26%, or 130,000, were *discs* of a remarkably similar appearance, usually described as "like two pie plates stuck together," with dimensions averaging some 50 feet in diameter, thickness about 10 feet.

In court 130,000 witnesses to a crime would most certainly condemn any criminal. In fact, just *one* incontestable eyewitness account can send a man to the electric chair.

On the score of circumstantial evidence it would seem that the sightings of 130,000 discs a year "proves" the flying saucer case. But there is more—much more.

There are many more *patterns* to be observed in repeated form from millions of sightings, adding much more weight to the circumstantial case for the UFO's.

Patterns

The wide variety of patterns to be explored will include three other things that came out in the report of Waldo J. Harris—metallic appearance, rocking motion while hovering, and tremendous speed. These, too, are an overwhelming common denominator in saucer sightings.

Again and again the UFO's are described as "metallic-looking," "shining like burnished silver," "like sand-blasted aluminum," etc., especially in daytime sightings with the sun glinting off their forms.

Second, the peculiar rocking motion Harris reported has been variously described by others as an undulatory, fluttering, or wobbling motion. While hovering, the object often rocks gently back and forth on its lateral axis. During horizontal flight, while still rocking laterally, the disc UFO's will also dip up and down in a wavelike motion through the air. When descending, they adopt a "falling leaf" pattern.

These are not isolated instances. Those motions are identically reported in thousands upon thousands of cases. Can a million people all hallucinate in the same way?

Third, on the score of speed as mentioned by Harris, almost *every* report—whether disc, globe, fireball, cigar, etc.—speaks of "fantastic" speed that no known earthly craft could match. In many cases reliable estimates range anywhere from mere supersonic speed up to 42,000 mph. The latter may seem unbelievable, but this figure came from three CAA control-tower operators at an airport, men technically trained to judge speed.

In the chapters ahead all these UFO "patterns" will be fully reviewed, culled from 20 years of sightings in America and around the world.

CHAPTER 2

Identified Flying Models

"On the afternoon of January 27, 1953," reported John B. Bean, "I was driving north (near Livermore, California), when I noticed a small, whitish object proceeding southward. . . .

"It began a shallow left turn, and at that point I could see it was perfectly round and had a metallic sheen. . . . Suddenly it began to alter direction, at first seemingly heading due south again, and then suddenly making a steep right-hand turn.

"It also began to climb at the most terrific rate of ascent that I have ever witnessed. . . . The interesting facts about this sighting were that I had three distinct types of aircraft (two F-86's and the UFO) within my sight range simultaneously. . . . There was no question that the disc-like object had far more power and far more rapid maneuverability than the other two (jets)." (Excerpted from *The UFO Evidence*, NICAP.)

THE ABOVE ACCOUNT is typical of the majority of sightings in that it deals with a *disc,* the most common UFO shape. The very first sighting since the "Saucer Age" began was that of Kenneth Arnold, who saw nine discs near Mt. Rainier on June 24, 1947.

When the shapes and physical characteristics of UFO's are examined, the pattern that emerges is very distinct indeed. At least 90% of all saucers seen can instantly be placed in well-known categories of shape that have repeated over and over, as can be seen from the following chart prepared by the NICAP.

Though based on a limited number of sightings, the NICAP percentage table below indicates the general breakdown of all UFO's as to shape:

COMMONLY REPORTED UFO TYPES

Note: These drawings are hypothetical constructions, generalized from hundreds of UFO reports. They are intended to indicate basic shapes which have been reported, and are not necessarily completely accurate in every detail. Additional details sometimes reported, such as "portholes," projections, body lights, etc., are not portrayed. The general types shown do represent with reasonable accuracy virtually all UFO's which have been reliably described in any detail. Examples of each type appear in the left-hand column.

UFO SHAPE	BOTTOM VIEW	BOTTOM ANGLE	SIDE VIEW
1. FLAT DISC A. 10-54 Cox 7-2-52 Newhouse B. 7-9-47 Johnson 7-14-52 Nash		A B oval	A B "lens- "coin- shaped" like"
2. DOMED DISC A. 9-21-58 Fitzgerald 4-24-62 Gasslein B. 5-11-50 Trent 8-7-52 Jansen		"hat- shaped"	"World War I helmet"
3. SATURN DISC (Double dome) A. 10-4-54 Salandin 1-16-58 Trindade 10-2-61 Harris B. 8-20-56 Moore	A elliptical or B "winged oval"	"diamond- shaped"	"Saturn-shaped"
4. HEMISPHER-ICAL DISC 9-24-59 Redmond 1-21-61 Pulliam 2-7-61 Walley		"parachute"	"mushroom" "half moon"
5. FLATTENED SPHERE 10-1-48 Gorman 4-27-50 Adickes 10-9-51 C.A.A.			sometimes with peak
6. SPHERICAL (Circular from all angles) 3-45 Delarof 1-20-52 Baller 10-12-61 Edwards	A metallic- appearing ball	B ball of glowing light	
7. ELLIPTICAL 12-20-58 Arboren 11-2-57 Lovelland 8-13-60 Carson	"football" "egg-shaped"		
8. TRIANGULAR 5-7-56 G.O.C. 5-22-60 Majorca			"tear-drop"
9 CYLINDRICAL (Rocket-like) 8-1-46 Puckett 7-23-48 Chiles	"cigar-shaped"	10. LIGHT SOURCE ONLY "star-like" or "planet-like"	

575 Sightings

Disc	149	26%
Round (spheres)	96	17%
Oval (elliptical)	77	13%
Triangular (wedge or tear-drop)	11	2%
Rocketlike (cigar)	48	8.3%
Light source (star-like)	140	24.3%
Other (no description)	35	6.1%
Radar observed (not visual)	19	3.3%

Reporting for the North American Newspaper Alliance, a wire service, top UFOlogist John Keel comes out with different percentages from his investigations:

504 cases

Disc	129	25.6%
Oval (globular)	33	6.6%
Cigar	27	5.3%
Starlike	287	57%
Other	28	5.5%

Despite the variations, it is noticeable that the discs still take up a good quarter of all sightings as in NICAP's table.

The disc may also account for many sightings of seemingly "round" or "oval" or even "football" saucers, as is apparent from the previous chart. Depending on the viewer's perspective, the disc may be seen as tilted to present an oval shape and tilted still more to become a football. Seen from directly underneath, the disc can also pass for a round "globe" if the sighter does not see it in any other position.

Hence, it seems likely that the discs predominate even more than the above table shows. However, the sightings have to be listed according to what the observer saw, often for only brief seconds under difficult lighting conditions.

Domed Discs

The second kind of disc—the "domed disc"—in NICAP's chart is much rarer than the predominant flat or lens-shaped type. But it does show up with enough frequency, from all parts of the country and the world, to be part of the mysterious pattern of UFO shapes that are definitely established as a "working model." As examples:

———December 5, 1954, North East, Pennsylvania, 1:40 to 1:50 A.M. A domed object giving off a brilliant orange glow was seen, with a double row of "windows" below the dome.

———November 5, 1957, New York, New York, 4:30 A.M. A domed disc hovered awhile, then sped away, bearing "portholes" on the dome.

———August 7, 1952, Kerkrade, Holland, early A.M. Two discs with flat domes were observed, both of them swooping, zigzagging, hovering, and performing other aerial maneuvers.

———June 14, 1958, Pueblo, Colorado, 10:46 A.M. Observed by a meteorologist was a domed disc 24.2° above horizon, altitude 30,000 feet, speed over 500 mph.

———August 13, 1947, Twin Falls, Idaho, 1:00 P.M. In Snake River Canyon a man and his two sons saw an object like "a broad-brimmed hat with a low crown" that followed the contours of the canyon and then vanished.

———May 11, 1950, McMinnville, Oregon, 7:30 P.M. On their farm the Trents saw a disc with a flat-topped dome on top, which hovered and "teetered" in the air 100 feet high for several minutes (see photos).

But if rare, the domed discs make up for it by the fantastic details that sometimes go with them. Try to picture the incredible vehicle that this young woman saw:

December 21, 1955, Washburn, Maine. Mrs. Roberta V. Jacobs, a young housewife, observed an unusual object low over her farmyard for six to eight minutes, around 11:00 P.M. She stated that:

"The shape was like a cup turned upside down on a saucer. . . . The color was like nothing I have ever seen, pure gold would be as close as I could say . . . I could see the flat bottom part going around and around real fast . . .

"Between the flat bottom part and the half-moon top there was something 'alive.' . . . I couldn't see any form or outline, but it was like a person walking in front of a light . . . like hurried movements.

"I felt as though 'they' had a telescope or something pointed at me . . ." (From *The Reference For Outstanding UFO Sighting Reports.*)

Saturn Discs

Category #3 in the NICAP chart, the Saturn disc, is a sort of double-domed type of UFO, seen more frequently than the single-domed disc. The Saturnlike ring around its middle is sometimes described as solid, sometimes as a glow, and in either case may be detached from actual contact with the parent body. These differences may be due simply to varied visual conditions, and perhaps the ring is always attached to the saucer, seeming separate only by an optical illusion.

When any two or more people see a jet plane in the distance and are unaware of its exact type, their descriptions, too, will often vary considerably. Some will see the tailpiece "detached" or even absent and the wings stubby or swept back when they really are not. In fact, witnesses of an accident between two cars often confound police by calling one car "big and black" when it really is small and dark green, and mention four doors when there are only two. And the vehicles may be only 50 feet away at the time of sighting.

How much less do we know about the actual shapes of UFO's!

Analogies may be dangerous, but to this writer, who has pored over thousands of sightings, it seems that the peripheral details of any broad type of UFO may be due entirely to subjective factors in the observer—the way *he* sees things.

If these are machines from a single or even several outer space worlds, it is more than likely that their various "models" are of a similar basic mold and do not display the *outré* discrepancies found in saucer reports. However, this is only an opinion that reinforces my general theme that UFO "patterns" repeat consistently and perhaps far more uniformly than we suspect from the confusing, undigested mass of sightings that have spilled forth for some 20 years without being duly sorted out and classified.

If this book can even partly eliminate some of the confusion, it will have served the purpose intended. It is my intention to *synthesize* and integrate sightings rather than "analyze" them, in the hope of adding some insight into the whole mystery of the UFO's.

One of the most famed sightings of the Saturnlike type of saucer is the Trinidade Isle report of February 21, 1958. The Brazilian training ship *Almirante Saldanha* had been converted into a floating laboratory to participate in the IGY experiments and studies of 1957–58. They were ready to observe weather balloons near tiny Trinidade Isle (not to be confused with Trinidad) in the South Atlantic when a flying object was spied coming over the mountains.

A quick-witted cameraman aboard managed to snap five photos as the UFO gyrated for about 30 seconds before speeding away. The Brazilian Navy has corroborated that the photos were genuine, although there was a later clampdown on all comments—which arouses more suspicions of the pictures' being authentic than otherwise.

At any rate, this is one of the fairly numerous Saturn-UFO's that have been reported. Herewith are other samples:

——October 4, 1954, Essex, England. A Saturn-shaped disc flew head-on toward an RAF plane, then veered off.

——March 9, 1954, Cincinnati, Ohio, 3:57 A.M. While driving, John H. Stewart saw a dark ellipsoid body encircled by a luminescent, pulsating halo, which hovered 7 or 8 minutes and then shot away, changing color from bluish white to yellow to molten red.

——February 2, 1955, Maiquetía-Merica, Venezuela, 11:15 A.M. An Aeropost Airlines plane came upon a round, glowing object, colored green, with a reddish ring around its middle and portholes above and below the ring. About to collide, the UFO veered sharply downward, then accelerated at an upward slant and vanished.

Hemispherical UFO's

The #4 type of disc in the NICAP chart is the "half-shell," or hemispherical, form, which is fairly common. It is often reported with portholes or windows and seems to be well lighted, sometimes shining forth searchlight beams. Note this typical sighting:

October 17, 1954, Varigney, France, 8:30 P.M. Motorists stopped on route D-10 when they spied a bright red luminous object in the fields. M. Beuclair and his daughter Jeanne walked closer, when suddenly the object moved and swooped toward them, coming within 60 feet.

Now they could see its peculiar form, a hemispherical body with a flat bottom. All at once, the Beuclairs reported, radiation burst out from the bottom in parallel streams of red and white.

"What is it?" yelled M. Beuclair in panic. "Who's there?" He had evidently presumed that someone was inside guiding the strange craft. There was no answer, and after a moment the eerie vehicle sped off at high speed. (From "The Reference.")

Spherical UFO's

Next in NICAP's chart are the round UFO's, or spheroids (17%), and the oval, or ellipsoid, saucers (13%). These can be taken together because they have many characteristics in common. These globes and "eggs" are presumed to be genuinely shaped that way, not being perspective views of discs.

Here is a typical account of a globular UFO plus the kind of incomprehensible maneuvers they display at times, leaving everyone gasping or shaking their heads in disbelief:

Summer 1952, Haneda Airport, Tokyo, Japan. At Haneda AFB, USAF personnel spied a brilliant light hanging over Tokyo Bay. Ground radar soon confirmed that it was a solid body.

Binoculars revealed that it was a lamp hanging from a huger dark spherical shape. When F-94's were sent to investigate, the UFO outmaneuvered them no matter what they tried. As if playing with them, the saucer made right-angle turns and impossible loops, often sidling up close to the planes and making the pilots sweat in alarm over a possible crash.

Several times the UFO audaciously approached the AFB radar tower itself, as if defying them to get a good "fix." At 12:03 A.M. the cat-and-mouse game was still going on, with an F-94 from Johnson AFB joining the act, only to find itself hopelessly outflown by the darting, twisting, sharp-turning UFO.

Finally, as if tiring of the "sport," the globular UFO simply piled on speed at an incredible rate of acceleration and left the jets as if they were glued to an invisible wall in the sky. Radar lost the saucer completely, and it was gone, leaving a mocking, silent echo at the air force base. (From *"The Reference."*)

One can only surmise from this report, and many similar ones, what would happen if the UFO's are here to make war on earth—which is unlikely, since they have had 20 years to start hostilities and haven't fired a shot yet. But in any contest or battle between the saucers and our jets earth's proudest air fleets would go down like falling leaves. And most likely not one UFO would be downed.

Oval UFO's

Switching now to the ovoid type, here is an interesting account from *The Reference For Outstanding UFO Sighting Reports* of the UFO INFORMATION RETRIEVAL CENTER, INC.:

November 4, 1957, Elmwood Park, Illinois. At 3:12 A.M. two policemen and a fireman were out in a squad car when they noticed a brightly luminous red-orange object "shaped like an egg" hovering over Elmwood Cemetery. It appeared to be about 200 feet long and was slowly descending as if about to land. Patrolman Clifford Schau, the driver, mistook it at first sight for the moon.

"I switched off our lights and started following it," said Schau. "When we got close, I turned the lights back on, and then it shot up about two hundred feet and went off in the west. I think it would have landed if we hadn't turned our lights on. We followed it for a while, at sixty-five miles an hour or more, but we couldn't catch it."

There are other puzzling details. Schau added, "I shone the big spotlight on the object, and the light almost went out," as if from some electromagnetic effect (see Chapter 6).

Patrolman Lukasek added that the object "seemed to be folding up like a parachute" until the spotlight beam struck it, when it "puffed out" again and sped off. (From *"The Reference."*)

Lest this deceive the casual reader, the UFO was not a parachute by any manner of means—not when it was chased for miles at 65 mph.

UFO Balls

There are several other aspects of the globular or elliptical UFO's that seem peculiar to them alone. Most of them are seen at night and often appear to be large "fireballs" of an orange or orange-red color. Some are reported to have "fuzzy edges" without sharp outlines.

Quite often they are seen to descend near the ground but seldom seem to actually land. In a good many cases they are the type of UFO that will chase cars, planes, ships at sea, and even people, as will be taken up in another chapter.

According to one theory by Jules Plantier, French engineer (revealed in *The Truth About the Flying Saucers* by Aimé Michel) these fuzzy fireballs may really be disc-shaped UFO's whose shape is camouflaged by its propulsion technique (see Chapter 5).

However, it seems likely that certain round or oval UFO's are just what they seem and nothing else, particularly when their shape is unmistakably seen under good visual conditions. Such are the following:

——August 23, 1960, Wichita, Kansas, 3:24 A.M. An aeronautical engineer and family saw a UFO like a big "Japanese lantern" with 3 triangular lights—or windows—that seemed to chase the Echo satellite for five minutes.

——August 30, 1965, Urbana, Illinois, 10:30 P.M.

Students saw a solid-looking ball, trailing a streak of light, which struck the pavement and bounced straight up into the sky, to vanish in seconds.

——September 1, 1958, Tripoli in Libya, North Africa, 10:15 P.M. Two technicians observed a bluish white globe descend until it was basketball-sized, then speed skyward again to star-size.

——October 26, 1958, bridge near Loch Raven Dam, north of Baltimore, 10:30 P.M. Two observers in a car saw a 100-foot-long ovoid hovering over the bridge, when it seemed to "explode" with a thunderclap, after which it was seen racing upward at terrific speed (corroborated by other independent witnesses).

——Summer, 1952, near MacDill AFB, Florida. A ground radar blip sent a B-29 to check, finding an oval-shaped glowing white ball at 40,000 feet, which completely reversed its field in a hairpin-U and then vanished.

——November 3, 1957, White Sands, New Mexico, 3:00 A.M. An Army jeep patrol spied an egg-shaped glowing UFO that descended slowly, brightened, and appeared to land but was never found.

Flat Spheres

The "flattened sphere"—#5 in NICAP's chart—is really a variation of the spheroid, and one typical sighting will suffice to indicate that it is related to the true spheres:

September 26, 1954, Chabeuil, France, 4:00 P.M. M. and Mme. Leboueuf went to gather mushrooms in the fields. In a wheatfield the woman screamed as she saw a three-foot-tall man in a "diving suit."

She ran and hid in a thicket. Peering out, she soon saw a big, metallic object, circular but rather flattened, rise up behind nearby trees with a slight whistling sound. Crossing the wheatfield at a low level, the UFO then veered northeast at tremendous speed.

After Mrs. Leboueuf called her husband and neighbors, they found a patch where shrubs had been flattened in a diameter of 11 feet. Bedded for three days with a nervous collapse, the woman described how two eyes had stared out of the diving suit's helmet at her, but they were "larger than human eyes," and the creature, whoever it was, walked with a waddling gait. (From *"The Reference."*)

This woman's story, most likely honest, is not to be confused with the "contactee's" elaborations. The contactee would go on and claim he talked telepathically with the little men, who invited him for a ride in their saucer and told him they were on earth to save us from nuclear war or to bring universal prosperity. Depending on the contactee's imagination and nerve, he might even baldly state they flew him back to Venus, their home world, and he saw a mighty civilization, etc., etc., etc.

Any "contact" cases used in this book are apparently authentic experiences in which people glimpsed "UFOnauts" stepping out of their landed saucers, but no words or any sort of communication were exchanged, and in most cases the saucerians quickly departed, as if wishing to avoid direct contact with earth people.

Triangular UFO's

Next in NICAP's chart come the "triangular" saucers, which are always sighted with rounded corners. There are such variations as the teardrop shape and the "flying wedge." From its low 2% rating, it is obviously the rarest type of all.

If we make the assumption that the saucers have arrived from outer space, they might come from *several* worlds rather than just one. Then, the triangular shaped UFO's might represent the craft of a "lesser" world that cannot afford to send large numbers of their particular model to earth, in contrast to the "rich" world that sends veritable fleets of the discs here.

On the other hand, the shape of any aerial craft would be based primarily on aerodynamic or propulsion factors that make the discs the most numerous simply because they are the most efficient for flying purposes in earth's atmosphere.

In that case, the flying "triangles" become hard to justify. Are they experimental models being tested? Do they serve some specific purpose or earth-observation mission that no other craft can perform? We do not know, and it is pointless to speculate.

Sample sightings of the triangular class follow:

———May 5, 1958, San Carlos, Uruguay. A UFO shaped like a top approached a plane and hovered, but when the pilot tried to close in, the object sped away at supersonic speed.

———July 24, 1952, near Carson Sink, Nevada. Two Pentagon colonels in a B-52 caught sight of three silvery, triangular UFO's that sped past at an estimated speed of 1,000 mph.

———March 23, 1960, Indianapolis, Indiana, 3:35 A.M. A metallurgist and wife observed a "kite-shaped" UFO, seemingly made of tiny glowing beads, that made turns of 180, 90, and 30 degrees, then reversed its course and vanished at high speed, estimated to be orbital speed (18,000 mph).

Cylindrical UFO's

This is the last, but very far from the least of the shapes in NICAP's UFO chart—the cylindrical or rocket-like UFO's, more often described as "cigars" or more rarely as "torpedoes."

Though comprising a modest 8.3% of the total, the flying cigars loom importantly in the hierarchy of saucers, for they are the famed "mother ships" of giant size, often seen with attendant craft that are smaller. For this reason, having "moonlets," they are more scientifically called the "satellite saucers."

These sightings of satellite saucers are one of the most telling *patterns* in UFOlogy, which almost seems to be proof in itself that the UFO's are from another world. It must be difficult indeed for the Air Force or any skeptical scientist to refute this if they once look over any of the best "cigar" sightings.

If visual evidence alone ever does crash the reality barrier, it will probably be the great mother ships that do the job. They are simply out-of-this-world at first glance, according to all eyewitnesses. And even reading about them gives one the eerie, spine-chilling feeling that these are uncanny craft never conceived of or made on earth but coming from some strange world of far greater technology.

Dr. Hynek, Dr. Condon, the Air Force, the French government, worldwide scientists—they must all have given pause to their skepticism if they read of the two satellite saucers sighted in France, which alone promote the reality of UFO's with tremendous impact.

Both cases occurred in France in 1952, within 10 days of each other and only a few miles apart. The verbatim reports alone even in shortened form, can make you, the reader, sit up in bewildered astonishment—because both events had *multiple witnesses,* up to a hundred people, who could not possibly all be liars, hallucinators, or town drunks. Judge for yourself. First, the report of M. Yves Prigent, general superintendent of the high school at Oloron, France, at 12:50 P.M., on Friday, October 17, 1952:

"In the north a cottony cloud of strange shape was floating against the blue sky. Above it a long, narrow cylinder, apparently inclined at a forty-five-degree angle, was slowly moving in a straight line toward the southwest.

"I estimated its altitude as two or three kilometers [about 1¼ to 1¾ miles]. The object was whitish, nonluminous, and very distinctly defined. A sort of plume of white smoke was escaping from its upper end.

"At the same distance in front of the cylinder about thirty other objects were following the same trajectory. To the naked eye they appeared as featureless balls resembling puffs of smoke. But with the help of opera glasses [which he had obtained] it was possible to make out a central red sphere [on each small object] surrounded by a sort of yellowish ring inclined at an angle [apparently Saturn-like UFO's].

"The(ir) angle was such as to conceal almost entirely the lower part of the central sphere, while revealing its upper surface. These 'saucers' moved in pairs, following a broken path characterized in general by rapid and short zigzags. When two saucers drew away from one another, a whitish streak like an electric arc was produced between them." (From *"The Reference."*)

Now the report from Tarn, in the Gaillac district, some 12 miles to the southwest, only 10 days later:

October 27, 1952, 5:00 P.M. Many residents, including two police officers and others, totaling over a hundred, were witnesses as a long, plumed cylinder inclined at a 45-degree angle flew over slowly to the southeast.

Surrounding this "mother ship" were some 20 smaller saucers, which flew two by two in rapid zigzags [sic]. In this case, however, some of the pairs of Saturnlike saucers left the herd and descended quite low over town, estimated to be [at height of] 300-400 meters [900-1,200 feet].

The spectacle lasted some 20 minutes before the "cigar" and its satellite saucers drifted out of sight over the horizon.

True Unknowns

Two groups of people in two separate communities, and ten days apart, observed a phenomenon remarkable for the close similarity of the two sightings. Both groups of multiple witnesses said:

They saw a giant cylinder shaped like a cigar.
The cylinder was at an angle of 45°.
The cylinder was attended by a group of Saturn-like saucers.
These saucers flew in pairs in rapid zigzag motion.

By no possible stretch of imagination, nor any conceivable conspiracy, could these two groups of honest French citizens have seen or concocted almost identical hallucinations or illusions of absolutely unorthodox and unearthly aspects. To suggest that the people of the two towns all suffered a common delusion or optical illusion is in utter violation of medical science or psychiatric knowledge.

Mirages? Cloud tricks? Hoaxes? None of those explanations seems remotely capable of accounting for this weird double sighting. The only logical conclusion must be that they are two genuine UFO reports of real objects.

Which leaves us with this haunting question echoing through the years—who or what appeared above Oloron and Gaillac in France in October 1952? And one is tempted to say that, putting the shoe on the other foot, this is one case where the authorities or skeptics must *disprove* what dozens and hundreds of reliable eyewitnesses saw, including public officials of the two towns.

The townspeople can hardly be asked to furnish "proof" in tangible form, outside of the evidence of their eyes in *broad daylight* during clear weather. It is, more logically, up to the anti-UFO contingent to prove that those people saw something *else* that is *not real*.

For if it is real, then at one stroke we have inferential proof that sentient beings of some sort—the pilots of the mother ship and its satellite vehicles—are visiting earth. *Where* they have come from is a different matter.

But with official or scientific attempts to discredit those two sightings totally lacking to this date, it stands that dozens of French people saw *some* kind of nonearthly vehicle sail over their two towns more than a decade ago.

Other "cigar" sightings and the mother-ship theory will be taken up in a future chapter, to add heavily to the circumstantial evidence piling up in favor of an extraterrestrial series of visitations that have occurred on earth for at least 20 years and more likely for hundreds or even thousands of years.

Ubiquitous Discs

In summary, one definite UFO "pattern" has emerged —their shapes fall into categories quite sharply distinguished from one another. And we might recall, as in Chapter 1, that an estimated total of 130,000 disc-shaped UFO's alone have been seen in the past 20 years all over earth. Not 130,000 different ones, of course, since each saucer will reappear time and again to new witnesses, often dozens or hundreds for the same UFO.

But even so, one begins to wonder just how *many* saucers are buzzing around earth when they are being seen daily at the rate of 57 per hour (see final chapter for statistical breakdown).

Discs, spheres, flying eggs, teardrops, cigars—these five broad categories of UFO's account for all but a small percentage of total saucer sightings. The "oddballs" that seem to fit no discernible pattern will be dealt with later, along with the starlike objects that have no describable shape.

CHAPTER 3

Miraculous Maneuvers

October 6, 1959, Lincoln, Nebraska. A U.S. Army Colonel, his wife, and their son saw an object making abrupt turns at high speed. The son had been studying astronomy and pointing out the stars. . . . His mother noticed the object and pointed it out. . . . At first they thought it was a meteor. It was round and . . . the color was between white and yellow.

The object was first seen 70° above the horizon at 15° azimuth (south-southeast). It moved north-northwest (330°) for about 12 miles and then made a quick turn north (360°), and . . . an abrupt turn east (90°). Shortly thereafter (½ mile) it made another abrupt turn south (180°). . . . It dimmed out and returned to bright(ness) several times. . . . (From *"The Reference."*)

THIS "WILD" REPORT has been given a 98 percent reliability quotient and is today still marked "unidentified," or unknown, by the U.S. Air Force. This sighting is typical of a large percentage of UFO reports and brings us to another special aspect of the saucers.

A major "pattern" among flying saucers is the kind of flight characteristics they exhibit and their astounding maneuvers in the sky. These aerial acrobatics are a "common denominator" repeated so many times by witnesses all around the world that by itself it removes the UFO's from the category of illusions and makes them a part of reality. It is similar to bird watchers who know all the flight characteristics of flocks of geese or waves of migrating birds, which fall into rigid patterns that seldom vary.

Almost every UFO witness seems most impressed and utterly dazzled by these antics, which no jet or rocket or flying machine produced on earth can come anywhere near to duplicating. The sky maneuvers of the UFO's are indeed "out of this world."

These incredible flight phenomena include the following:

Fantastic speeds through the thickest air near earth's surface.

Enormous acceleration, from hovering to blistering velocity.

Straight-up flight at almost immeasurable speed.

Descent by means of a peculiar "falling leaf" maneuver.

"Impossible" right-angle turns without slowing down.

Hovering with a "rocking" or teetering motion.

Forward flight in zigzag or wave-motion undulations.

Circling in tight, high-g turns impossible to humans.

Collision courses with planes, ending in dead stops in midair.

UFO "dogfights" together in crazy darts and twists.

Erratic "sky dances" carried on by solo saucers.

Fleets of UFO's flying in perfect formation at high speed.

Saucers "splitting" into two or more vehicles.

Saucers "joining" into one vehicle in midair.

There are other strange movements and gyrations the UFO's go through at times, all of them entirely beyond the capability of any earthly plane. Most witnesses call the UFO maneuvers they see "eerie" and awe-inspiring.

Speed and Acceleration

——May 29, 1950, near Washington, D.C. An elliptical UFO circled an airliner, hovered awhile, then sped east at "fantastic speed."

——June 30, 1950, near Kingman, Kansas. A rotating saucer hovered over a minister's car, then took off with terrific acceleration.

——June 1, 1952, Los Angeles, California. A target UFO, being tracked by radar at 11,000 feet, suddenly tripled its speed and climbed rapidly at the rate of 35,000 feet per minute.

——July 14, 1952, Chesapeake Bay near Norfolk,

Virginia. Six red coin-shaped objects sped silently past an airliner, piloted by William B. Nash and William H. Fortenberry, at an estimated speed of 12,000 mph.

——April 24, 1949, White Sands Proving Grounds, New Mexico. Four Navy technical personnel tracking weather balloons spied a fast-moving distant object in their theodolite (tracking telescope). The UFO was estimated to be 56 miles high and going 25,000 mph (the escape velocity from earth) yet without leaving orbit.

——Summer 1952, Terre Haute, Indiana. Three CAA control-tower operators at the airport saw a saucer streak across the sky and, assuming that its height was over 3,000 feet, came up with the incomprehensible speed of 42,000 mph. That it was lower in altitude seemed unlikely, and if it were higher up, it was going even faster. This, so far, is the highest estimated speed of a UFO, made by highly trained men familiar with all flying craft known.

Whether hovering, loafing along, abruptly departing like a cannon shot, reaching gasping velocity, turning tight circles, it all seems to be child's play to the amazing flying saucers.

Straight-up Flight

One of the most ubiquitous maneuvers reported about UFO's is their ability to achieve vertical ascent at blinding velocity, as per the cases ahead:

——July 10, 1947, Southern New Mexico. An astronomer saw an elliptical UFO hover and wobble, then make a "remarkably sudden ascent" estimated at 600 to 900 mph.

——January 20, 1951, near Sioux City, Iowa. A rocketlike object flew alongside a DC-3 and suddenly shot up out of sight.

——January 17, 1956, Orangeville, Canada. A flying disc hovered, moved horizontally, then shot upward in a spiraling motion, vanishing in 5 or 6 seconds.

——July 22, 1952, New Smyrna Beach, Florida. A

metallic disc hovered 10 seconds, then shot away in an abrupt fast climb.

——December 20, 1958, Dunellen, New Jersey. Police saw a bright red oval UFO come from the west, hover a bit, then "zoom straight up like a shot."

——August 24, 1959, near Emmitsburg, Maryland. A brilliant white planetlike UFO hovered for 2 minutes, then took off straight up at terrific speed.

It has been suggested by Major Donald Keyhoe, among others, that these craft, after completing some observation mission below, are shooting back up to their mother ship, which is hanging invisibly high.

Right-angle Turns

As in the first sighting at the start of this chapter, this eye-bugging maneuver of sharp-angle turns is displayed by saucer after saucer. It, too, is a unique characteristic of the majority of reported UFO's. Other cases:

——June 28, 1947, Maxwell AFB, Alabama. Two pilots and two intelligence officers of the Air Force saw a starlike object zigzagging with bursts of speed and making a 90-degree turn.

——July 3, 1954, Albuquerque, New Mexico. Nine round, green-glowing UFO's hovered, then turned 340° at about 2,600 mph.

Even more startling than sharp turns, perhaps, are those UFO's that reverse their course without the slightest change in speed, like a Yo-Yo suddenly being pulled back:

——Summer 1952, MacDill AFB, Florida. A colonel piloting a B-29 observed a glowing ellipse that reversed its direction (180°) and sped away.

If living creatures are aboard such craft, how can they possibly survive the crushing g-loads—1,000 g's or more —that would result from such abrupt changes of direction? Even if the craft are unmanned and automated, how can any structure withstand a wrenching force that would rip any earthly jet into shreds? A theory to cover this inexplicable phenomenon is taken up in a later chapter on UFO propulsion.

There are many other cases of UFO's performing another feat impossible in our aerodynamic concepts—flying tight circles around a jet or an airliner that no rudder or wing-flap system we know could possibly accomplish. The saucers literally "fly rings" around our fastest and most maneuverable jets.

Pilots have reported trying to turn "inside" the UFO only to come close to blacking out from angular g-forces. When their eyes cleared, there was the UFO mockingly turning inside *their* course with lazy ease. Pilots have sworn it's impossible, yet they saw it happen hundreds of times. It is no freak occurrence but another oft-repeated "pattern" of the sometimes maddening UFO's.

UFO "Dogfights"

This is one of the strangest maneuvers the saucers indulge in, for it seems to make no sense whatsoever.

Two or more UFO's will dart and weave and loop around one another for no apparent reason. But whether we understand why they do things or not, these are still valid "patterns" of their observed behavior. Perhaps someday we will know the answer to such baffling mysteries. The dogfight maneuvers are well documented, as in the following examples:

———August 3, 1952, Hamilton AFB, California. Two silver discs wove around each other, then were joined by 6 more, whereupon they all took up a diamond formation and flew away.

———November 16, 1948, Japan. Air Force radar detected two UFO's maneuvering, like planes in a dogfight, for over an hour.

Quite often, for no known reason, the UFO's "playfully" get into dogfights with jets, though no weapon is ever used by the saucerians. The jet pilots have to sweat it out until it's over, realizing that if the UFO had a gun, it could easily shoot down the clumsy earth planes. For example:

———August 12, 1953, Rapid City, South Dakota. A UFO first fled from a jet, then came back and maneuvered around it as if in a dogfight or playing a cat-

and-mouse game, fleeing each time the jet turned for a closer approach.

————August 23, 1955, Cincinnati, Ohio. SAC radar watched three jets engage in a bloodless dogfight with three circular UFO's that later sped away.

————December 11, 1955, near Jacksonville, Florida. Navy jets were in a nonshooting dogfight with one UFO that outmaneuvered them all, confirmed by radar.

UFO Targets

It is said on good authority (Donald Keyhoe among others) that the Air Force has secretly given its jet fighter pilots orders to shoot at any UFO within range. If true, it is unquestionably the most idiotic and dangerous course we could follow against an obviously superior "enemy" —if enemy they are.

To open fire rather than try to establish friendly relations is a sad and damning commentary on the state of "civilization" we boast about.

True, it is the mission of the United States Air Force to defend this country and shoot down or drive away any "unauthorized" craft, which can be interpreted to mean any vehicles from outerspace as well as from across the seas. But since the UFO's have made no overt hostile moves, at least on a large scale, should it not be presumed that theirs is a *friendly* mission of one sort or another?

It is related that a tribe of savage Amazon Indians, upon first sighting a low-flying plane, immediately began hurling their futile spears and arrows at it. The pilots shook their heads wryly at such ignorant idiots opening fire on what were obviously highly advanced—and peaceful—newcomers.

We can assume that the saucerians, if they exist, find us the same "ignorant savages" who fire first and ask questions later. And certainly the USAF has no inside information yet that there are no saucerians within the mysterious saucers.

Fortunately we can all breathe more easily because

there are no firm indications that an earth plane has ever been shot down by a UFO, or vice versa. Quite obviously, because of advanced technologies beyond our wildest drawing-board dreams, the UFO's are *invulnerable* to our weapons, just as they are safe from ever being run down by the clumsy contraptions we fly.

The sheer effrontery of our hoping to defeat or capture a machine of such superscientific people is only exceeded by our arrogance in assuming that earth people are at the acme of intelligence and science technology in the universe—an attitude more rampant among scientists than laymen, according to the few open-minded scientists who accept the UFO phenomenon as real.

Whether earth will adopt a saner and more sober attitude toward our possible visitors from galactic worlds and substitute welcome messages for gunfire remains to be seen. So far we have reacted to the unknown in unreasoning stupidity. And let us hope that by sheer mischance one of our jet aces does not succeed in knocking down a saucer and killing its crew.

Retaliation might be as swift and devastating as if we had prodded a cosmic snake.

Fleet Formations

Another enigmatic aspect of the UFO phenomenon is the appearance of small or large flocks of UFO's flying together as if on some mission. Again, these multi-UFO "fleets" appear often enough to constitute a distinct pattern, even if we are unaware of the motive behind grouped saucer flights.

UFO's have been seen traveling in pairs, threes, fours, and on up the number scale to startling squadrons. Ten or more UFO's together are not uncommon sightings, as in the following:

——August 1, 1952, Albuquerque, New Mexico. A Scripps-Howard staff writer observed 10 UFO's that shifted formation with absolute precision, from a cluster to a V, then to rows of two abreast, all at great speed.

——March 24, 1954, Baltimore, Maryland. A civil

defense official witnessed 14 UFO's in a V-formation first, which changed to a single-file line when an airliner passed below.

———August 28, 1954, Oklahoma City, Okla. Hundreds of people stared up and clearly saw a flight of 15 saucers in a V-formation that switched to a semicircle when pursued, leaving the jets far behind.

———August 2–3, 1965, from South Dakota to and beyond the Mexican border. Uncounted thousands of people in eight states were awed when for two nights saucers flew over in wave after wave, hundreds of them in all. This is the most massive sighting of grouped UFO's ever recorded, totally unexplained to this day, authenticated by radar at a half dozen Air Force bases and by photos taken by civilians.

Sometimes the actions of smaller groups is quite as mystifying, as in the following cases:

———January 5, 1958, Beechwood, Ohio. A housewife reported 3 UFO's that first rotated around one another as if at the corners of a triangle, then split up and sped in three different directions.

———April 9, 1958, Cleveland, Ohio. A family observed a flight of 9 UFO's that suddenly separated into two groups of 4 and 5.

From these last two reports we can see that the UFO's carry on many strange and unknown tasks or missions, some of which require fleets to split up. But more startling than a fleet splitting up is when a saucer itself seems to split apart.

Splitting and Joining Saucers

—April 11, 1964, Homer, New York, 6:30 P.M. Dr. Warren B. Ochsner, physiotherapist, his wife, and two children were having a picnic. First they saw a cloudlike object that behaved strangely. Nearby they saw a saucer, "and then the most incredible part occurred—from the saucer shape it became almost perfectly round and slowly divided into two parts, one above the other, very much as a single cell does under a microscope. The top object slowly became smaller as it appeared to fade off in the distance, while the second object headed downward at a forty-five-degree angle . . ."

—Mid-August, 1951, Central, New Mexico, 10:30 A.M. Alford Roos, mining engineer, looked up, and "there were two objects (that converged), at which time they were in close proximity. . . . Over Fort Bayard there was an isolated cloud-island covering perhaps three degrees of arc and perhaps a mile across. The two objects shot straight up at this (previous) steep angle at incredible speed, both entering the cloud, and neither appeared beyond . . ." (Excerpts from *"The Reference."*)

Can we even attempt any educated guesses as to just what these phenomena represent? We can but with hardly any assurance.

The splitting saucers in the first case might be similar to our two-stage rockets or boosters, the spent stage being jettisoned as it burns out. However, in the case of the UFO's, they hardly "burn out," for each of the "segments" seems to be a new craft able to fly by itself.

The joining saucers of the second case are something we've never duplicated with our rockets during rapid flight but only by slow jockeying in orbital rendezvous and docking operations, so that UFO maneuver is something beyond our knowledge. One might hazard the supposition that if a saucer meets propulsion trouble, it "joins" with one or several others in order to be hauled away or repaired. Or if one of the UFO's seems larger than the others, it might be a lesser version of the giant mother ships that were mentioned in Chapter 2.

More likely, all such saucer activities are for reasons entirely beyond anything we know and are totally unrelated to what they seem to be—the "splitting" and "joining" of UFO's.

Erratic Solo Saucers

Very baffling, too, are single saucers that engage in the wildest and weirdest "sky dance" imaginable. This kind of UFO will indulge in eye-popping maneuvers all over the sky, as if "showing off" to the earthlings below, although they indubitably have a more serious purpose.

It might, though implausibly, be a saucer that went out

of control, with the UFOnaut crew within desperately
trying to tame their wild steed. But the fact that none of
these erratics seem to crash—at least no wreckage has
ever been found—suggests some other explanation, one
that we cannot provide at this time.

Here is a typical case of the crazy-quilt solo saucer
flights:

July 30, 1962, Ocean Springs, Mississippi, nighttime. A
seafood salesman and family . . . observed a large, bright,
cherry-red object . . . moving very slowly from right to left
at   treetop   level   and   sometimes   appearing   to   be
stationary . . .

The object began to make half loops very fast as it continued to move right to left. It would go straight up, move over
a degree or so, and come straight down. . . . It was moving
in a square-wave pattern. . . . It would go up, across, and
down in less than a second

After returning approximately to the starting position, it
paused, then moved very fast horizontally from 100° azimuth
to 95° azimuth. . . . After this flash back and forth it would
continue to move to the left, making square-wave movements, then reversing and repeating, staying between 8° and
15° above the horizon. . . . (From *"The Reference."*)

Other solo flights are more erratic, including zigzags
across the sky, sudden stops and starts, and all sorts of
haphazard motions in any direction at any speed. A chart
made of one such UFO's movements came out as a confused mass of twisted lines such as a child might scrawl
on a slate.

Undulatory Flight

Here we come to the most significant of all characteristics of UFO's in flight, for it is repeated far more often
than any other feature and is, in the main, peculiar to the
largest UFO group—the discs. There must be millions of
cases if all sightings around the world for 20 years are included.

The chart on page 41 shows that the phenomenon is divided into several parts that are related to the rocking
characteristic (courtesy of NICAP):

A) The satellite objects of a mother ship revolve in

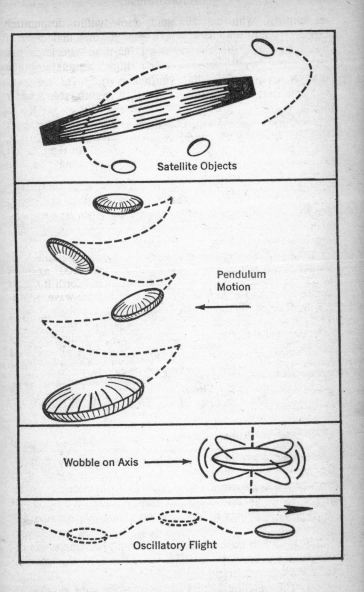

Satellite Objects

Pendulum Motion

Wobble on Axis

Oscillatory Flight

various ways. This will be taken up in detail in a later chapter.

B) The UFO uses a spiraling motion to gain altitude and a "falling leaf" pattern to lose altitude.

C) When hovering, the disc-saucer *rocks* (or teeters, sways, undulates, wobbles, etc., all meaning the same thing).

D) During flight the UFO will either zigzag horizontally or weave vertically in a wavelike path.

Falling Leaf Pattern

Remarkably consistent, described over and over the same way by countless witnesses, is the "falling leaf" (or "dead leaf") manner of a UFO's losing altitude when it wants to descend a short way. This is often during the time it is approaching the ground for a landing, or for low-level and treetop flight. Outstanding examples are:

——September 26, 1954, Col du Chat, France. Fifteen people saw a disc like an "inverted plate" that was descending "like a falling leaf."

——February 24, 1958, Salvador. Three people observed a hemispherical UFO descend from 90 feet to 9 feet above the ground by imitating a "falling leaf."

——September 20, 1952, Topcliffe, Yorkshire, England. Following a Meteor-Jet, a silvery disc descended with a "pendulum motion."

——July 1957, Azusa, California. A disc-shaped UFO with a row of amber lights on its rim descended with a "wobbling motion."

——December 25, 1960, Cottonwood, Minnesota. A family observed a hemispherical ball slowly flutter down like a "falling leaf."

For some reason that may have to do with their propulsion (see chapter ahead), UFO's sometimes adopt a spiraling motion to gain altitude, the reverse of the falling leaf descent. But this maneuver is rare enough to be unimportant.

Wobbling

This is the greatest single flight characteristic, as noted

before. The witness in the following case was obviously greatly impressed by the "rocking chair" motion of the UFO he saw:

September 1950, off the coast of Korea. Three fighter-bombers took off from a U.S. aircraft carrier. Their mission was to strafe an enemy truck convoy in North Korea. Reaching land, they searched the ground below, and one pilot was "startled to see two large circular shadows coming along the ground from the northwest at a high rate of speed."

He continues: "I looked up and saw the objects which were causing them. They were huge . . . going at a good clip . . . about a thousand or twelve hundred miles an hour. . . . The objects suddenly seemed to halt, back up, and begin a 'jittering' or 'fibrillating' motion."

His radar inexplicably became jammed, and his radio blacked out while "the objects were still jittering up there ahead of us, maintaining our speed. . . . They were at least six hundred or possibly seven hundred feet in diameter.

"The objects had a 'silvered' appearance, with a reddish glow around them. . . . In the middle of the underside was a circular area, coal black and nonreflective. . . . And it is important to note that although the whole object 'jittered' while maneuvering, the black circular portion on the bottom was steady . . ." (From *"The Reference."*)

To cite a tiny fraction of the many other sightings where this "jittering" or rocking motion was observed, note the following:

——July 6, 1947, Fairfield-Suisan AFB, California. An Air Force pilot saw a UFO "oscillating on its lateral axis."

——July 10, 1947, Southern New Mexico. An elliptical UFO (probably a disc seen at an angle) was sighted by an astronomer and "wobbled" while hovering.

——August 14, 1952, Coral Gables, Florida. A luminous object with an orange ring around it hovered and wobbled back and forth every few seconds.

——September 9, 1952, Portland, Oregon. Two oval, or disc-shaped, UFO's hovered, and one of them wobbled.

——July 26, 1955, Washington, D.C. A round UFO approached an airport, then hovered and oscillated before speeding away.

———August 15, 1957, Woodland Hills, California. A disc hovered for 6 minutes, rocking from side to side, then rose straight up out of sight.

———November 29, 1957, Sarasota, Florida. A round orange object wobbled and hovered for 2 minutes, then moved.

———May 5, 1958, San Carlos, Uruguay. A brilliant top-shaped UFO approached and stopped, rocking twice before speeding away.

———July 27, 1966, Chattanooga, Tennessee (courtesy *Saucer Scoop*, Vol 1, #6, September 1966, written and produced by Joan Whritenour and Jean Chapman, St. Petersburg, Florida). Randy Vincent, driving back to his home in Orlando, Florida, states: "In the late afternoon, as we drove southward . . . I spotted a dark, disc-shaped object with a knob on the top and bottom, wobbling as it rose vertically in the west. It stopped and hovered briefly, then started moving south with an up-and-down motion . . ."

Other Flight Characteristics

Coming to the zigzag horizontal flight displayed by some saucers during flight, this can either be an angular type of movement or a smooth "snake-wriggle" motion, as the following cases will indicate:

———January 10, 1958, New Orleans, Louisiana. An orange light-source zigzagged across a lake at high speed.

———April 11, 1958, South Africa. A white and red light-source moved back and forth in a steady 30-degree arc (when not hovering).

———August 3, 1958, Ontario, Canada. A starlike light sped west to east, zigzagged in several directions, then continued east.

———January 10, 1961, Benjamin, Texas. A starlike UFO in zigzag flight appeared to land.

Then, there is the vertical wavelike motion, akin to the way dolphins dive in and out of the water, as in these cases:

——March 20, 1956, Washington, D.C. Three discs, tilted in a wobbling motion, also moved up and down (during flight).

——July 7, 1947, near Medford, Oregon. A disc on edge moved south to north along the eastern horizon, bouncing up and down "as if following the contour of (invisible) hills."

——May 29, 1951. A large formation of glowing UFO's maneuvered and moved with undulatory "skipping" motion.

It is to be noted that the very first publicized sighting, by Kenneth Arnold in 1947, mentioned that the nine discs he saw were like saucers "skipping" across the water, displaying the up-and-down motion so often seen later.

Fantastic Flight

In summary, the flight-maneuver pattern for UFO's is very specific and widespread, and is one of the strongest circumstantial points offered in proof of their reality. When enough people see the same thing repeated in widely scattered areas around earth and in widely scattered calendar periods from 1947 to date, it can no longer be called a subjective or illusionary phenomenon but must be something decidedly real.

Fantastic speed, incredible acceleration, impossible turns, straight-up flight, precise fleet formations, the various undulatory motions—all these must be a telltale result of the special aerodynamic and propulsive techniques employed by the UFOnauts.

Just *what* it all means in terms of craft structure and power plant we don't know and can only guess at blindly. But the *pattern* inherent in saucer maneuvers is undeniable and becomes another pillar in the case for the existence of UFO's.

CHAPTER 4

They Come in all Colors

June 18, also July 2, 3, 1965, at South Pole stations of Britain, Argentina, and Chile. For 20 minutes 19 Antarctic scientists watched a gigantic UFO, shaped like a double convex lens, go through amazing gyrations in the sky—zigzagging, going at high speed and stopping dead, hovering for a minute at a time, and changing speed and direction often.

It was glowing all the time and changing color. Red and green were its predominant hues, but it also exhibited shades of yellow, orange, blue, and white.

Their consensus was that no earth-made machine existed or could exist of such a shape and displaying such incredible velocities and mobility in space. (Condensed from *"The Reference."*)

WIDELY REPORTED, THESE color changes are another highly significant saucer pattern. They are described so often in the *same way* that it in itself is tantamount to proof that the somethings up there are solid and real, not the illusions of deluded people or ordinary objects mistaken for UFO's.

A large majority of saucers seen during the daytime are said to be silvery, white, or grayish, sometimes with a faint colored halo or glow around them. But at night the UFO's flash forth in their true rainbow glory, exhibiting every color known and various shades of each.

Some nighttime UFO's do not seem to change color, although this may be mostly in the case of very brief sightings. To indicate the wide variety of monocolored UFO's that are seen, NICAP has broken down their own and the Air Force's reports as follows:

Night or Twilight	NICAP (575 Cases)		Air Force* (2199 Cases)	
Red	62	10.8%	179	8.1%
Orange	25	4.3%	221	10.1%
Yellow	28	4.9%	159	7.2%
Green	21	3.7%	144	6.5%
Blue	26	4.5%	93	4.2%
Purple	0	0.0%	5	.2%

There is some discrepancy in the red and orange cases in these breakdowns, which may be due merely to different techniques employed in gathering information from observers.

These all represent starlike lights, bigger globes and ovals, fireballs, and fuzzy luminous objects of various sizes, which appear the same color throughout the sighting, although the intensity of their light may vary.

Further typical examples are:

——February 7, 1953, Korea. An F-94 pilot spied a bright orange light that changed altitude and pulled away at high speed.

——May 12, 1957, near La Sal, Utah. Lt. Col. Samuel E. Craig, an Army flyer, observed a round, blue-green object below his plane.

——January 26, 1952, Fairchild AFB, Washington. A blue-white spherical object sped overhead, speed computed at 1,400 mph.

——July 26, 1952, Washington, D.C. An F-94 pilot chased a large yellow-orange light.

——October 7, 1959, near Forrest City, Arkansas. An Air National Guard pilot pursued a glowing white UFO.

——March 1944, Carlsbad, New Mexico. A high-speed, glowing green object lit up a pilot's cockpit, moving out of sight over the horizon.

This last sighting is in the category of *green fireballs*, a

(* Project Blue Book Special Report No. 14, page 143, table A65)

special kind of UFO that will be taken up in a later chapter.

Color Changes

Now we come to a different and more spectacular category—the UFO's (still mostly seen in the nighttime) that *change* colors.

Here a remarkable pattern emerges in which the color changes are almost certainly related to the UFO's movements—hovering, speeding up, slowing down, descending, ascending, and high-speed acceleration.

A rough scale would relate the colors to motions in this way:

White when hovering or moving at uniform speed.

Red and *orange* when accelerating.

Blue or *blue-white* at extremely high speeds.

Green when making right-angle turns or performing other aerial maneuvers.

Not all sightings will neatly fall into those pigeonholes. Often these color sequences are violated or occur in a different order. However, a theory has been worked out that relates the colors to *energy* changes rather than mere speed changes. For example, a UFO may turn from white to red while still hovering because it is building up a "power load" in order to accelerate, after which it will remain red.

Another theory ties in the amount of air-friction *heat* generated by the UFO with its altitude so that it might be blue-hot at lower heights and merely red-hot high up in thin air, even though accelerating at the same rate in both cases.

Still another possibility is that ionization effects around the UFO because of its electromagnetic (presumed) propulsion system could play many color melodies on the radiation spectrum's octaves.

However, it is not speculation but established fact from multiple sightings that the color changes are exhibited with *motion* of the UFO's, as these cases ahead will show:

———November 27, 1950, Huron, South Dakota. Airport technical personnel watched a UFO that alter-

The object in the foreground appeared over Perth, Australia, and was photographed by Mr. L. Benedek. The curving row of lights is the waterfront of Perth.

"Saucer nest," or landing spot of a UFO, near Tully, Queensland, Australia.

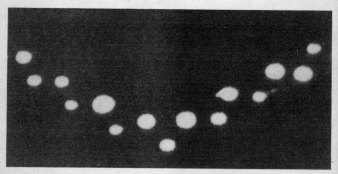

The famed Lubbock (Texas) Lights, photographed in 1951 by Carl Hart, Jr. Observers estimated that the lights were 50,000 feet in the air and moving at 18,000 mph.

One of the famed Trinidade Isle series of photos of a UFO. Taken aboard a vessel of the Brazilian navy close to shore.

One of a series of photos taken by Paul A. Villa, Jr., on June 16, 1963, near Albuquerque, New Mexico. This is among the clearest pictures of a UFO ever taken. Some authorities have declared this photo and its mates to be hoaxes, but other experts maintain that they are genuine.

A UFO circling a seaplane base.

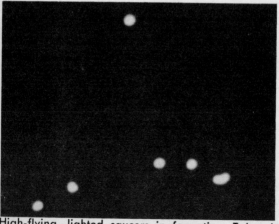

High-flying, lighted saucers in formation. Taken by Robert Stevens, in 1956.

nately hovered and darted around the sky, changing color from red to white to green.

———November 6, 1957, near Danville, Illinois. Two state policemen chased a brilliant white light that changed to amber and orange.

———May 18, 1963, New Plymouth, New Zealand. A university student saw a fuzzy glow that made speed dashes across the sky, changing color repeatedly from white to red to blue.

———November 25, 1956, Pierre, South Dakota. A sheriff and a patrolman chased a luminous object that kept changing to different shades of green, red, and white as it moved or remained stationary in the sky.

———November 14, 1953, near Toledo, Ohio. Civil Defense Ground Observer Corpsmen saw a glowing UFO flash forth orange, white, blue, and red colors.

———August 7, 1963, near Fairfield, Illinois. Two men spied a yellow-orange diamond-shaped object that changed color to bright orange, then gray, and finally blue-white.

———Reporting on the Ontario, Canada, flap of spring 1966 (*Saucers, Space & Science* #43, Summer 1966) Gene Duplantier compiled no less than 21 sightings in which spectacular color changes were exhibited by UFO's, often ranging through every portion of the spectrum—white, red, orange, green, blue, gold, and all shades in between. For some reason, saucers displaying amazing color changes seemed to concentrate in that area through the spring of 1966.

Beacon Lights

So far we have really been dealing with UFO's glowing from within or glowing all around their structure. There is another class of saucers that seem to carry intense lights, and this is what the observer sees rather than its true form, which is hidden by the glare.

Airplane pilots often report lights hung on vague shadowy shapes that they cannot make out. It would seem that for some reason this class of UFO's is equipped with beacon lights, either steady or blinking, and sometimes with searchlights that cast a bright light over the ground below when they fly low.

Typical of these beacon-carrying UFO's are the following:

——July 12, 1952, Chicago, Illinois. A weatherman saw a reddish object with small white body lights that made a 180-degree turn and vanished over the horizon.

——August 5, 1952, Oneida AFB, Japan. Control tower operators watched a dark, circular UFO with a brilliant white light mounted on top.

——December 29, 1952, North Japan. USAF personnel spied a UFO with rotating red, green, and white lights, plus 3 fixed white lights.

——1955, near Washington, D.C. A missile expert observed a dark disc with a lighted dome on top.

——October 5, 1950, near San Fernando, California. A UFO with body lights made a pass at an airliner and dipped below it.

——December 8, 1952, Chicago, Illinois. An airline pilot saw a string of 5 white lights and a 6th red one blinking rapidly, apparently attached to a UFO.

Most UFO's seen after dark and described as *starlike* are probably just the attached lights aboard a saucer, seen at a distance, with the actual body invisible to the eye. The following cases would fall into this pattern:

——December 27, 1950, near Bradsford, Illinois. A TWA pilot saw a light-source only, making erratic and violent maneuvers.

——May 22, 1951, near Dodge City, Kansas. A blue-white starlike object moved up and down, back and forth, then dove under a plane and vanished.

——July 13, 1952, near Washington, D.C. A bright light-source approached a plane, hovered then fled when the pilot turned on his landing lights.

——January 30, 1953, near Yuma, Arizona. A gyrating light ascended steeply in the sky.

Unorthodox UFO's

Finally there is a small but spectacular group of UFO's lit up like gaudy floats at a nighttime parade, displaying a bewildering variety of light phenomena. No two are alike. They seem to bear little, if any, relationship to one another. Each is individually and independently lit up, so that for once we have no pattern at all to go by. It is as though out of earthly aircraft that display certain fundamental characteristics—fuselage, wings, prop or jet, tailpieces, landing gear—we suddenly met Rube Goldberg flying devices that have totally different aerodynamic forms. Ahead are a few examples (all excerpted from *"The Reference."*) of such "maverick" UFO's whose lighting characteristics are bafflingly unorthodox:

——July/August 1955 (date indeterminate), Willoughy, Ohio. This is the story of W. M. Sheneman, a radio-TV store proprietor, as he was returning home one night with his wife and his children.

"I saw a red light about a thousand or eight hundred feet away. . . . The ground was illuminated with two brilliant lights. . . . I realized this was no airplane or anything I had ever seen before. I yelled back at my wife (at the back door), 'Hell, no, don't turn on any light.' . . . My wife and children were all crying 'What is it, Daddy? What is it?'

"This thing was now over my garage, about fifty to a hundred feet off the ground, hovering there. . . . A big red light in the front and a big green light on the rear. . . . We could make out the outline of a dome affair on top. It was lit up with a lot of tiny lights inside . . . I would say it was about eighty to a hundred feet in diameter and was flat at the bottom.

"It hovered over the edge of the woods approximately five minutes, then it seemed to drift away."

——September 14, 1963, off Oporto, Portugal, seen from aboard a ship, as told by Second Officer Knud Rasmussen:

"An unidentified flying object appeared, bearing two hundred ten degrees. . . . Coming closer, the object

appeared as a brilliant green light. . . . There was a
faint green and orange tail. . . . Ahead of the green
light were ten to fifteen orange or red lights. . . . But
they seemed to be changing positions. The only two
lights that seemed to keep the same distance from each
other were the green and purple lights."

————June 8, 1964, Lawrenceville, Illinois. Living on
a farm outside town, Mrs. Helen Reed saw a UFO descend close to her barn.

"After it stopped," she reported, "I suddenly noticed
that its yellow lights were rotating counterclockwise.
The speed of rotation increased to very high rpm, and
at the same time they (the lights) were all as if on a
vertical band moving from left to right at low rpm. Evidently at one place there was a wider space, as if a
light was missing. Twice I saw that space go by."

Monstrous machines, indeed, as if out of disordered
dreams. Yet all the witnesses swore by what they had
seen and signed statements. What they represent and why
they should be so different from the "regular" UFO's simply cannot be answered or even conjectured.

Still, we must remember that when our own astronauts
land on the moon and Mars, they will use specialized vehicles and machines that look different from one another,
each engineered to fit its specific mission best.

Similarly, the saucerians would require a wide variety
of vehicles to explore all of earth's complexities in the
most efficient way. Those big craft with many odd lights
might be surface-observing machines with special sensors
and instrumentation.

Lighting Phenomena

Another possibility, of course, is that the UFOnauts
are not necessarily from one outer space world but several, perhaps even dozens—a heterogeneous band of explorers from various civilized worlds all making up a single team, just as during the IGY we had international
scientists working together. If they differ in physical form
and have different technological histories, their vehicles

would not be the same types.

At any rate, some of the low-flying craft reported have been among the most *outré* of all, with a perplexing array of lamps, beams, searchlights, and flashers.

These do not by any means exhaust all variations of the light phenomena featured by UFO's. Reported sporadically rather than widely are such puzzling optical effects as:

—A white-shining UFO trailing a red flame.

—Saucers with pulsating lights that dim and brighten rapidly.

Newark, New Jersey, 1964: many in this neighborhood saw this craft, with strange halo effect.

—UFO's surrounded by glowing "halos" or "clouds."

—Saucers, usually cigar-shaped, that have rows of lighted portholes.

—UFO's that give off explosive showers of colored sparks.

—Saucers with rotating light-sources, somewhat like police cars.

However, all anomalous specimens aside, perhaps 80% of the UFO's seen at night are "normally" lighted and display that strange pattern of color changes related to motion.

Any given UFO does not just hover and change from white to orange to red to blue to green. It adopts new colors only when it moves in some way. Why?

Many investigators believe that the rainbow display of colors bears a direct relationship to the UFO's *propulsion* system and, in fact, is a clue to what amazing kind of engine and force drives them at such blistering speeds and in such dizzying maneuvers. This will be taken up in the next chapter.

CHAPTER 5

Way-Out Propulsion

April 24, 1964, near Socorro, New Mexico, from the account of police officer Lonnie Zamora after he had come upon an egg-shaped vehicle parked near a shack:

. . . He had hardly turned around from the police car when he heard a roar. . . . It was not exactly a blast but a very loud roar. It was not like a jet. . . . It started quickly at low frequency, then rose in frequency and loudness. . . . Simultaneously he saw flame under the object. . . . It was blue and orange. There was no smoke. . . .

Zamora turned to run and fell. "Being that there was no roar (now)," he said, "I looked up and saw the object going away from me. . . . I heard a sharp whine from high tone to low tone. . . . Then there was complete silence.

"It disappeared as it went over the mountain (at 120 mph). It had no flame whatsoever (at this time) as it was traveling over the ground, and no smoke or noise." (From *"The Reference."*)

THIS ACCOUNT FROM one of the most reliable of all UFO witnesses is perhaps our only slight clue to the propulsion system of flying saucers. It is interesting that the roar was totally unlike a rocket's takeoff except for a minor burst of flame.

But the sound was evidently some kind of engine noise, changing from low to high frequency, followed by the whine. And after its initial burst of flame at takeoff from the ground there was no further sound or flame. It then moved silently, as most UFO's are reported to do, although one might assume that the whining sound continues but is too low-pitched to be heard except at very close range.

Other UFO's have made takeoffs remarkably similar to this case:

——November 6, 1957, Dunn, North Carolina. Lester E. Bee, a minister, saw a bright circular object rise straight up, giving off a flash of light and making a sharp, explosive sound.

——October 26, 1958, Baltimore, Maryland. Philip Small and Alvin Cohen witnessed a huge egg-shaped object hovering low over a bridge, when it suddenly rose rapidly, giving off a bright light and a flash of heat, and making an explosive sound.

Distant UFO's always move silently, according to observers. But those accosted at close range—on the ground or at treetop level—are reported with sound effects. We can dismiss various "whoosh" and "swish" noises as these would probably represent the sound of any big object moving through the air and creating a backwash of wind.

The other sounds, which seem to be internal, are the ones that may be a clue to what unknown power plant drives the UFO's. Note these cases:

——December 14, 1963, near Vereeniging, South Africa. Two men heard a "gentle hum" from a UFO as it hovered over their stopped car.

——April 8, 1950, River Road, Texas. A boy saw a small saucer land, but when he approached, it made a "whistling noise" and took off.

——Spring 1952, Hasselbach, Saxony, Germany. A man and his daughter saw a UFO on the ground that made a "slight hum" and rose upward.

——September 10, 1954, Quarouble, France. When a man came upon a UFO hovering just over the ground, "a thick dark steam was coming out of the bottom with a low whistling sound." Then the craft went up.

Electromagnetic Clue

The oft-reported "hum" or "whine" or "whistle," which may be the same thing, suggest something entirely different from the combustion engine or jet engine, which together run many of our machines and vehicles. It reminds one immediately of the electric motor, which leads us into the fields of magnetism, electromagnetism, and perhaps gravity.

We must now rid our minds of all preconceived notions about propulsive power as we know it. The maneuvers of the saucers in the sky are absolutely "impossible" in terms of any engine we know or have even theorized about.

But, then, the combustion engine was just as "impossible" to the horse-powered middle ages, and the electric motor was a revolutionary device when it was introduced, based on Faraday's studies of magnetic fields and electrical phenomena.

The principle of the rocket, based on Newton's third law of action-reaction, was thought to be of little use until big missiles grew from the small pioneering rockets of Robert Goddard. Today the spurned "reaction engine" is driving our giant rockets out into space.

The laser, the fuel cell, and the thermionic "battery" are the newest and most advanced power sources, based on the intricate physics of the nuclear-and-space age, and would have been "impossible" in the eyes of any scientist only a few years ago.

It is no more than common sense, then, to recognize the fact that we ourselves will hit upon even more amazing motive-power concepts that are inconceivable today. Whatever powers the UFO's is just such an unborn paragon of motive technology that may not come up in our earthly progress for many years. Hence, it will seem "impossible" at first glance and probably draw the withering scorn of any scientist—the same withering scorn that the scientist of the 17th century would have given to the steam engine. Scientists, unfortunately, tend to deny the possibility of anything beyond the body of knowledge they are masters of. All else is "science fiction" or sheer poppycock.

As one open-minded scientist put it. "We tend to project our own science technology into the future as a limiting factor, failing to make room for an unknown technology yet to be born."

And if science has not by now learned that the impossibility of today is the commonplace of tomorrow, then human progress is in for a bad fall. The great "law of breakthrough," all through history, has operated to bring forth science discoveries that were never foreseen.

Along with this is the great probability that out of millions of inhabited worlds out in the cosmos many thousands will be far more advanced than earth is, in the ratio of modern science compared to the Stone Age. If earth's 300-year uprise of science technology has been extended to 3,000 or 30,000 years on other worlds, the imagination boggles at what immense heights could be reached in the mastery of space, energy, and matter.

UFO Propulsion

Granted, then, that the power plant within UFO's is something entirely inconceivable, even preposterous, to our earth-limited science technology. Whatever it is, it must utilize forces we have never tapped or even dreamed existed except in very vague and frowned-upon theory of the "science fiction" type.

The answer, according to engineers and scientists who have made exhaustive studies of UFO phenomena, can be broadly encompassed in the term *electromagnetic power*. This in itself is too generalized to mean much and it means different things to different investigators.

Electromagnetic power is envisioned in several ways, as follows:

A) *The antimagnetic drive,* in which interactions with the earth's magnetic field are skillfully manipulated.

B) *The hydromagnetic* (*hot plasma*) *engine,* in which forces akin to thermonuclear fusion are harnessed to interact with earth's ionized air.

C) *The g-field or unified-field energy,* wherein gravity itself can be manipulated through electromagnetic means.

D) *Plantier's force field,* in which the intergalactic magnetic fields that generate cosmic rays are utilized as an intangible "fuel."

In all of these, note the common denominator—*mag-*

Photo of strangely lighted craft taken in 1965 by James Lucci of Beaver, Pennsylvania.

netism or *electromagnetism*.

We have learned in the space age many surprising things about electromagnetic phenomena on an interplanetary scale, among them being:

—That earth's magnetic field extends much farther than was thought, a "tail" of it even going beyond the moon.

—That huge and powerful magnetic fields exist in "empty" space *between* the planets.

—That the sun creates a "solar wind" in space composed of electromagnetic particles and forces of super-hurricane power.

—That besides gravitation, strong electromagnetic forces clash and interact between the sun and the planets, little of which we understand yet.

—That circling the earth around its equator is a "doughnut" of subatomic particles displaying many electromagnetic properties — namely, the well-known Van Allen Belt.

Again the major factor in all these discoveries is *electromagnetism,* which in brief means the energy field produced by certain reactions between magnetism and electricity. It all stems from the area of *nuclear and particle physics,* which we have just begun to explore. Locked up in the tiny hearts of atoms lies some giant of power even greater than atomic fission or fusion that manifests itself as electromagnetism and pervades all the universe both within the fiery cores of stars and throughout the vast gulfs between them.

The light that reaches us from an unthinkably remote star is one form of *electromagnetic* radiation, with the ability to pierce billions of light-years, or quintillions of miles, of space. X-rays, ultraviolet and infrared radiation, and also radio and radar are all the offshoot of *electromagnetic* reactions in the form of energy waves.

Slowly science is growing aware that the classical Newtonian concept of gravitation "ruling" the universe does not hold up by itself and that mighty electromagnetic energies operate throughout every inch of the cosmos in ways yet unknown.

Antimagnetic Drive

The main exponent of the antimagnetic drive was the late Wilbert B. Smith (died 1962), a Canadian engineer who had been put in charge of Canada's Project Magnet in 1949, which was organized by the government to study UFO's seriously.

Basically his idea was that the saucers used a magnetic "sink" to trap earth's magnetic field, producing enormous power when the lines of force were cut by the craft. Cutting the lines of force of any magnet can produce power, as witness the electric generator that whirls a coil across the lines of a magnetic field and converts kinetic energy into electricity.

Smith was able to show that, just as the aurora borealis is a rainbow-hued phenomenon associated with earth's magnetic field, the movement of UFO's through the earth's lines of force would also produce the various shades of orange, red, yellow, blue, green, and white exhibited by the saucers. He could also account for the UFO's ubiquitous "wobbling" when hovering as due to the constant fluctuations of earth's magnetic field, so that the saucerian pilots constantly had to keep their antimagnetic forces in balance with the planetary field around them.

However, there were two major flaws in his concept. One was that the heat of air friction during high-speed flight could be dissipated only by rapid rotation of a ring, dome, rim, or some whirling part of the saucer. Though some UFO's are seen to spin and whirl, in part or in whole, no such motion was discerned in the majority of sightings.

Second, Smith's theory allowed for the amazing right-angle turns and other incredible maneuvers of UFO's but did not in any way ease the enormous g-loads that would result. Hence, he had to postulate that all fast-moving UFO's were automated and contained no living beings. But the evidence of "intelligent control" in many saucer sightings, especially when jets had "dogfights" with UFO's, is too strong to allow for too many pilotless UFO's sailing in our skies.

A variant of this magnetic manipulating system is presented by Brinsley le Poer Trench (*The Flying Saucer Story*), in which he suggests that the UFOnauts control the forces from two mighty magnetic "generators"—the sun and the earth.

He speculates that by the piezo-electric effect—using semiconductors as amplifiers of electricity—these giant interplanetary fields of magnetism are made to produce electromagnetic power of astonishing force, accounting for all the hyperhorsepower flight characteristics of the UFO's.

Also, in *Mars the New Frontier* Wells Alan Webb has come up with a third thought—that the UFO operators apply the Faraday Effect (polarized light in a magnetic field) to earthly and interplanetary magnetic fields to provide motive power.

All of these "antimagnetic" concepts smack too much

of "projecting our technology" into that of the UFOnauts, as though our science has really discovered all the principles necessary for creating a UFO-type engine—which is very doubtful.

Plasma Engine

Regarding the hydromagnetic, or hot-plasma, theory, Le Poer Trench briefly suggests the possibility that instead of natural space magnetism, the UFO technologists have harnessed *artificial* electromagnetic power of nuclear proportions out of the atomic fusion effect (H-bomb principle).

Hans Lauritzen of Denmark (in *Flying Saucers,* #51, March 1967) carries this concept a bit further by dealing with cold instead of hot plasmas of ultrathin ionized gases. The cold plasma could be made superconductive at cryogenic (ultracold) temperatures and produce great power endlessly in giant frozen magnetic coils.

Lauritzen has also advanced a theory that UFO's might use some sort of "bootstrap" mechanical system of springs that can be beefed up to produce all the megahorsepower forces needed to gyrate through the skies (*Saucer News,* #66, Winter 1966–67).

Again, this concept seems a "graft" of our technology onto a technology that is far beyond such "primitive" principles.

It is far more likely that UFOnaut technology has long since abandoned hydromagnetic plasmas, thermonuclear reactions, gigawatt laser jets, or any other concept we know, along with the steam engine and the gas burner, and has probably gone beyond the next three big steps we will make in motive power, too.

A more imaginative concept for UFO power can be mentioned in passing—using vacuum technology to fly around while in earth's atmosphere, if not in airless space.

The vacuum conditions produced are vaguely attributed, by the author, to the use of "cathode rays." But, granting that vacuums could be created instantaneously in the outside atmosphere around a saucer to any degree from "soft" to "hard," the craft would then create a continuous "vacuum tunnel" ahead of it and be driven forward by air pressure from behind.

Sound in principle, the concept sounds difficult to achieve in practice, with perhaps not enough flexibility in flight dynamics to account for the unrestricted movements of saucers. It is much more likely that the UFO power plant is a supremely *simple* device with a minimum of hardware controlling macro power.

We come now to the two main propulsive possibilities that seem the most valid—the gravity and the force-field concepts.

They are alike in one significant way. Both of them eliminate or suspend the normal laws of inertia *within the saucer* to allow for UFOnauts to withstand body-crushing g-turns and shipwrecking stops and starts with no trouble at all.

G-Field Control

The gravitic approach is sponsored by Professor Hermann Oberth, famed "father of space travel," whose theoretical and engineering equations led directly to the V-2 rocket and all space launchers of both Russia and America.

In essence, Professor Oberth's concept is that each UFO creates its own *private gravitational field,* which immediately makes it independent of earth's gravity pull so that it can easily hover and achieve high speed at will.

In addition, his idea allows for controlled interactions with earthly gravity to pile on acceleration to any degree and in any direction relative to earth—a distinct feature of UFO maneuvers.

The greatest virtue of the g-field drive is that it would automatically make all parts and persons within the craft subject only to its internal gravity, not to earth's gravity. That is, every atom and molecule aboard the UFO is within this protective cocoon of independent gravity and goes with it routinely regardless of outside conditions or forces.

Therefore, the UFO and its pilots are not subject at all to the formerly inescapable law of acceleration in earth's gravity field. Nor do the UFOnauts have any earth "weight," since there is no outside "pull" on their bodies.

In effect, they are in weightless "free fall," quite like the astronauts in orbit but right down on earth. For that reason the craft can make an abrupt right-angle turn without any g-effects such as all inhabitants of earth must suffer if they try it. Every atom of a saucerian's body, within the UFO's own g-field, turns with that g-field. Earth has lost its grip and its power to affect the craft at all.

The g-field also neatly accounts for the utter silence—except perhaps for the low whine of its g-field generators—of UFO's in flight, for the air around the saucers is *dragged along* instead of roaring past them. For the same reason there is no heating by air friction, and the craft remains cool despite speeds of 5,000 or 10,000 mph through earth's dense air, which would melt and vaporize any known metal or alloy on earth, and destroy any ingenious ceramic-plastic ablative material such as those used in the heat shields of our manned spacecraft.

As for the spectrum of colors displayed by saucers, Oberth believes that this comes from the power plant's manipulative g-forces that convert short rays into long rays to release power—that is, from the violet end of the visible spectrum to the red end. Each particular movement of the UFO—hovering, acceleration, sharp turns, high speed—would result in a color change as the electromagnetic vibrations that produce colors change frequency and wavelength.

Amplifying this point, Paul Norman (in *The Australian Flying Saucer Review,* #2, October 1964) says: "The influence of gravity on light has been pointed out by astronomers as they observe the stars. Therefore, the g-field of the flying saucer is variable and strong enough to affect the frequency of the light-waves, which explains both gravity control and color change of the object."

All in all, Oberth's artificial g-field concept seems to cover all the mysterious phenomena of UFO flight. All that need be granted is that such a g-field can be produced—a thought at which most orthodox scientists today would snort, no doubt. But not if they stopped projecting earth's halting technology to the grand technology mastered by the UFOnauts.

Perhaps some "Einstein" tomorrow—or a century from now—will stumble on the basic equation, as simple as $E = MC^2$ for atomic energy, for the creation of the laboratory g-field.

Incidentally, it is significant that Einstein himself kept seeking the "unified field" equation, which would link up all known forces and energies into one neat bundle—including gravitation and electromagnetism. Such an equation would point the way to *conversion* of gravity into electromagnetism, just as matter is converted into energy in the atomic bomb.

This leads us directly into the final UFO propulsion theory and the one that seems closest to the mark.

Electromagnetic Force Field

There is one other thing besides a g-field that can counteract earth's gravity field around a UFO—another kind of force-field, just so it is *stronger* than gravity. And such a force-field already exists, even if in weak form, around every natural magnet or electromagnet on earth. Creating a magnetic force-field that is powerful enough to negate gravity should be simply a matter of increased power input.

In 1953 Lieutenant Jules Plantier, an engineer of the French Air Force, began working out a theory of electromagnetic propulsion for space vehicles without, at the time, thinking of UFO's. It was only after he had developed his concept and worked out the engineering formulas that he suddenly realized they all applied perfectly to flying saucers. In fact, miraculously so.

As explained by Aimé Michel in his book, *The Truth*

About Flying Saucers, Plantier used the following premises:

—That distributed throughout space in all the macrocosmos is a form of high-powered energy, one of whose manifestations is to create the well-known cosmic rays of immense power.

—That this great and all-pervading energy, available between the stars, can be liberated or converted into a motive force for spacecraft—or UFO's.

—That liberating this cosmic energy, which streams right down to earth's surface, creates a *local* electromagnetic field that can be varied and applied at will, accounting for all the flight phenomena associated with UFO's.

Like Oberth's gravitic theory, the *EM-field* in a UFO cancels out earth's gravity, drags the surrounding air with it, and exhibits color changes that are the side effects of the clash between gravitation and the EM force-field.

But Plantier's theory is more precise in that it can show mathematically just why rapid acceleration should produce *red* light, or high-speed turns *green* light, or hovering a *white* glow.

He is also able to account superbly for the famed "falling leaf" descent of UFO's. Instead of turning their power up or down, the UFO pilots simply tilt their EM-field at an angle to earth's gravity field, which *lessens* the repulsion force between the two fields. This lets gravity pull them down a few yards at a time so there is no danger of dropping like a stone. Stepping power up and down might result in too fast a drop for the UFOnaut to pull out in time, especially when close to the ground.

Plantier's calculations can even explain why the giant cigar-shaped mother ships hang at an angle, why a corona or halo effect sometimes surrounds the saucer, and why some UFO's have rotating and whirling rims or domes.

He also worked out the reason why UFO's have dogfights. They are really maneuvers to allow one saucer to "reorient" its EM-field, which is "askew," or sometimes to allow for "refueling" operations in which invisible power is transferred between two saucers, accompanied by an "explosion" and pyrotechnic effects, which are often reported in sightings.

But most telling of all is that Plantier's EM power plant for UFO's explains all the EM effects reported by observers—car motors stalled, radios blacking out, and the burning "rays" or "paralysis" some people have felt in the proximity of a saucer (see next chapter).

Universal Power

Plantier's ingenious concept is not really tacking earth technology onto an unknown UFO technology, for no "electromagnetic engine" has yet been made or designed on earth. It is the kind of "pure research" concept that has all the earmarks of a breakthrough in scientific thinking, which is "proved" more or less by the loud laughter that greets the EM-drive from scientific authority. It has been called "fanciful," "impossible," "utter bilge"—the approximate terms that greeted the first airplane of the Wright Brothers.

Furthermore, his basic premise rests on scientific faith only, that the entire universe is filled with a new and unknown kind of electromagnetic energy spilled out by blazing stars and pulsating galaxies. This is Plantier's extrapolation from the fact that space age research has already revealed amazing electromagnetic forces right within our own solar system and more of it with each passing year and orbited probe.

This energy-crammed universe has all the dramatic impact of an intuitive scientific insight, the kind that has always struck the lightning in fertile minds to give us our greatest wonders—X-rays, atom smashers, DNA, antibiotics, radar, and all the other breakthroughs of science.

But whether Plantier is close to the mark or not, it can safely be stated that UFO propulsion must use some type of "universal fuel" in the form of energy that is extracted from a well we have yet to discover on earth.

CHAPTER 6

Electromagnetic Wizardry

"We were taking a ride out near Loch Raven Dam (north of Baltimore) Sunday, October 26 (1958). . . . We took this left-hand turn and we saw, from that distance, what appeared to be a large, flat sort of egg-shaped object hanging between a hundred and a hundred fifty feet off the top of the superstructure of the bridge over the lake.

"When we got to within seventy-five to eighty feet of the bridge, the car went completely dead on us. It seemed as though the electrical system was affected; the dash lights went out, the headlights went out, the motor went dead. . . ."

This man's companion, who was driving the car, gave his own account: "When we first saw the object, it was approximately three hundred yards away. . . . We slowed down to approximately ten or twelve mph and came to within seventy to eighty feet of the object.

"The electrical system in the car seemingly gave out, as if you had your points go up or somebody took the battery out of the car. . . . I tried to put the ignition system on but there was no whirring or anything. I put the brakes on the car, and we just looked at the object. . . ."

There were further experiences involving lights from the UFO, an explosive effect, and other phenomena, and then, "After it disappeared from sight, we came back into the car and turned the ignition system on, and it immediately went into operation. . . ." (From *"The Reference."*)

This is one example of another pattern displayed by the UFO's—the widely reported phenomena of *electromagnetic effects* when a flying saucer is nearby. Some sort of field of energy, probably related to the ship's propulsion, seems to surround UFO's with effects that are various and startling:

Killing car motors
Blacking out radios or causing static
Interfering with TV reception
Affecting compasses and other instruments
Stopping electric clocks and wristwatches
Jamming radar
Blacking out power stations

Even more alarming are the physiological effects on human beings themselves—"flashes" of heat, skin-burn from "rays," temporary "paralysis"—but more on this in the next chapter.

A NICAP analysis of 110 sightings of low-flying or landed UFO's indicates that about one-third of such close-contact experiences are accompanied by some kind of electromagnetic effect.

The Air Force has constantly reiterated that if a car motor stalls, it is because the witness in his excitement at seeing a UFO kills the engine himself. But when this happens in *thousands* of worldwide cases, as it has, one can hardly picture *that* many nervous drivers killing their engines. And the Air Force is usually pregnantly silent about those cases where the car's engine stalls, the radio stops playing, and the headlights go out, plus perhaps the witness's hearing a high-pitched whine or hum from a low-flying saucer and maybe feeling his skin tingling in "hot flashes." All these mechanical and physiological effects at the same time can hardly be dreamed up by people, but the Air Force has a low regard indeed for the veracity of the American people.

Other EM Effects

The bewildering variety of EM effects can be readily seen from these brief reports:

———August 28, 1945, near Iwo Jima. A C-46 had engine trouble and lost altitude as three UFO's were observed.

———June 24, 1947, Cascade Mountains, Oregon. A

ranger's compass needle waved wildly as a UFO passed overhead.

———September 1950, Korea. When two large discs approached Navy planes, the planes' radar jammed, and their radio transmitter was blocked by buzzing noises each time a new frequency was tried.

———September 29, 1953, East, Pennsylvania. A family reported their TV picture "going up and down real fast" as a UFO emitting white vapor flew overhead.

———August 30, 1954, Pôrto Alegre, Brazil. House lights failed as a UFO passed by.

———October 14, 1954, near Brosses-Thillot, France. Motorcycle stalled when a round, lighted UFO was seen 50 yards ahead.

———June 26, 1955, Washington, D.C. National airport ceiling lights went out as a round UFO approached; the UFO was caught in searchlight beam, then searchlight went out.

———November 16, 1956, Lemmon, South Dakota. Railroad phones and automatic block system went mysteriously dead as a UFO sailed over the yards.

———November 5, 1957, Philadelphia, Pennsylvania. A couple's apartment lights went out, and their electric clock stopped as a flaming disc passed overhead.

———January 30, 1950, near Lima, Peru. When a UFO hovered over a truck, a bus, and a car, the motors of all three vehicles failed.

EM Oddities

Those are the more prosaic effects. But even eerier EM phenomena have occurred, among which are the following:

———October 23, 1954, Cincinnati, Ohio. In one home the radio made harsh, shrieking sounds, and the volume increased as a reddish disc circled above.

———October 1956, Olso, Norway. A motorist felt a "prickly sensation," and a jeweler later told him that his wristwatch had been magnetized.

———April 14, 1957, Vins-Sur-Caraney, France. As a UFO maneuvered in the sky, metal signs vibrated and became magnetized.

———November 3 or 4, 1957, Araranguá, Brazil. An airliner's direction finder and transmitter-receiver set were burnt during a UFO sighting.

———November 6, 1957, north of Ottawa, Canada. A battery-powered shortwave radio failed, then a single tone signal was heard on one shortwave frequency while a UFO passed over.

———November 7, 1957, near Orogrande, New Mexico. A motorist's speedometer waved wildly between 60 and 110 mph when a UFO was observed.

An odd thing about EM effects is their apparent *selectivity* at times, whether deliberate or inherent in the interfering EM field. Note the contradictory effects in the cases ahead:

———November 14, 1954, Forli, Italy. A conventional (gas-powered) and Diesel tractor were driving side by side as a luminous UFO flew past, causing only the conventional tractor to stall, while the Diesel kept going.

———October 22, 1959, Cumberland, Maryland. A hovering UFO caused a car's motor, headlights, and radio to fail.

———February 9, 1962, Ashton, Clinton, England. A passing UFO made a car's motor lose power, but the headlights were unaffected.

There are many inconsistent cases where a car's motor, headlights, and radio will all three be affected, or only two, or sometimes only one. From this and other selectivity cases Brinsley le Poer Trench advances the theory that this is the saucerian's way of "signaling" us and showing us that the UFO's we see are intelligently controlled. Any natural force-field would act blindly and always black out everything within range. Only beams of energy delicately controlled can blink out a light and leave a radio working by the proper selection of interfering waves.

However, like all speculations about the riddles riding in our skies, there may be some entirely different reason and some undiscovered *pattern* that accounts for the weird workings of the EM effects.

Electrical Blackouts

The above cases are all relatively trivial, seldom if ever causing any harm or long distress to people. But now we come to one specific EM effect that is much bigger in scope and may have serious significance of some kind. The following cases will build up the pattern:

(Data from George D. Fawcett, noted UFO authority.)

——November 14, 1957, Tamaroa, Illinois. Just after a hovering UFO flashed brightly, power failed in a four-mile area for ten minutes.

——November 25, 1957, Mogi-Mirim, Brazil. All city lights failed as three UFO's passed overhead.

——August 3, 1958, Rome, Italy. As a luminous UFO was observed, city lights went out in a large area.

——June 22, 1959, Salta, Argentina. City lights blacked out as a luminous UFO sailed by.

——August 17, 1959, Uberlandia, Minas Gerais, Brazil. In this celebrated case that touched off hysteria a round UFO was seen following a power trunk line, whereupon automatic keys at the power station turned off, plunging the region into darkness; the keys turned back on by themselves after the UFO left, and there was no damage to the circuits.

Whole towns, communities, and cities deprived of lights and electrical power for a short period of time when UFO's flew over—what is the meaning of it? And is there some meaning in this fact, which was pointed out by J. J. Robinson of "S.A.U.C.E.R.S." and *Saucer News,* that during the greatest blackout of all of the Northeast United States in November of 1965, at least 23 UFO's were sighted throughout that area? This blackout plunged most of eight states and two Canadian provinces into darkness when the main electrical "grid" system failed. Many long and harrowing hours went by before the power came back on, city by city, for 30 million people groping in the dark.

To date, no firm or official statement has come forth to account for the big blackout, neither from the government or the power utilities. Several "theories" were advanced, then withdrawn. And it was finally stated that there was no assurance that it would not happen again, as if some agency *beyond their control* had generated the power blackout.

True to this prediction, even if on a lesser scale, most of the state of New Jersey was "blacked out" (during the daytime) on June 5, 1967, for several hours. Again, nobody knew *why* . . . unless we hear that saucers were sighted that morning near power plants.

If the UFO's did deliberately cause the blackout, what was their purpose? As a test of how to "subdue" earth when the time came, since our civilization would grind to a halt without electricity? Or simply as a scientific experiment to see what made our power system tick?

EM Patterns

The late Professor Charles A. Maney, head of the physics department of Defiance College, Ohio, in a book (*The Challenge of UFO's* coauthored by Richard Hall, Acting Director of NICAP) analyzed and tabulated various EM effects to give a more comprehensive picture of this UFO phenomenon.

Table I   Statistics based on 81 cases

Equipment affected	*Number*
Ground vehicles (autos 43, other 6)	49
Radio and TV (excluding car radios)	16
Aircraft (engines, lights, radio, radar)	7
Building lights	7
Other	2

Table II   Statistics based on 43 cases (autos only)

Part affected	*Number*
Motor only	12

Radio only 7
Lights only 3
Motor and lights 15
Motor and radio 3
Motor, lights, and radio 1
Other 2

Motors, total involved 31
Lights,   "   "   19
Radios,   "   "   13

The largest single incident involving EM effects on cars occurred on November 2, 1957, near Levelland, Texas, when one UFO—seen by 15 witnesses—caused four cars and trucks to stall, their headlights also going out.

Oddly, the colors of the UFO's in a series of EM effects included every possible kind—blue, green, white, red, orange-yellow, and multicolored (almost evenly). This does not necessarily indicate that the EM effects were not directly related to the UFO's presumed electromagnetic engine, where the colors would be a function of the engine's operation. Whether the UFO is hovering and "idling" with a white color or accelerating into its fiery red phase, the force-field of the EM drive is constantly around it, causing the EM effects in any case on nearby earthly vehicles and electrical systems.

In the case of radio and TV effects, there are four basic types of EM interference:

—Instrument goes dead, complete blackout.

—Volume changes, usually diminishing.

—Static is heard, varying from "noise" to "beeps" to "howls."

—Strange "signals" are picked up, often reminiscent of Morse code.

The last item strongly indicates that the affected set is picking up intercom signals between UFO's, which are undoubtedly in communication with one another at all times. No one has yet deciphered any of the signals received into a sense-making pattern, so it does not seem likely that the saucerians were trying to contact us.

Ultra-Power of UFO's

This point, of course, is one more of the baffling enigmas behind the UFO's, not only why they are here, but why they don't contact us? Some UFOlogists believe that after two decades they are still trying to master our language or languages. And if our astronauts reached Mars and found a living civilization there, it might well take them 20 years or more to master an alien tongue purely from listening to their broadcasts.

One thing becomes apparent from the EM effects of UFO's. Car radios, engine electrical systems, and lights are not affected to any great degree by our most powerful radio transmitters or TV broadcasts, or by passing close to huge power plants and radar installations, and for the Soviets to jam our Radio Free Europe broadcasts requires a string of antennas and stations pouring forth megawatts of power.

An energy-field that can jam radio, black out lights, and stall motors from distances of 50 feet to perhaps 1,-000 feet must be of immense power beyond anything our engineers can pack in an apparatus only 50 feet wide—or even 50 miles wide.

In short, if the UFO's propulsion system utilizes some form of electromagnetic power, that power must be measured in *gigawatts* (giga = billion). This is hardly a surprise when we think of the gargantuan power it must take for a UFO to accelerate from zero to 5,000 mph or more, as they often do, and vanish from sight in seconds.

The power plant within a single UFO no doubt holds the awesome power to light up every city in America or outpull all the combined jets in SAC or tow a hundred ocean liners around the world.

It must, in fact, be something akin to thermonuclear power equal to a stockpile of H-bombs, all housed and quietly tamed within one small craft to perform prodigies of flight. Or it may be a new kind of power yet unknown to us—Plantier's cosmic energy, antimatter fuel, quasar-type ultraenergy, who knows what?

Certain it is that not one jet has ever outflown a flying

saucer, and not one of our clumsy rockets can come even close to the gasping acceleration the UFO easily attains. Nor is there anything on our drawing boards—many engineers and scientists swear this—even remotely capable of the staggering flight performance of these flying question marks above us every day and night, all over the world.

Super Technology

Probably every government on earth has a secret project in which top brains are frantically trying to find the breakthrough to UFO propulsion (if we assume that governments deny UFO's only *publicly*). Somebody may stumble on it tomorrow. Or it may elude our primitive technology and scientific understanding for another century or a thousand years.

We may be seeing the technology of earth in the year 5000 flying over our heads today, achieved by a world that has had science technology for a longer time than it took ape-man to evolve into mankind.

We may be as totally *outclassed* by these deep-space visitors as we ourselves outclass the hive-building bees and mound-making ants. They, too, may be as futilely proud of their "engineering achievements" in hives and mounds as we are of our jets and rockets, which the saucerians may class with obsolete machines they had in their "prehistoric" times.

The electromagnetic effects we have reviewed may be the sign of a revelation that will crush all human pride in the dirt once we know by what fantastic power plants they are generated.

EM effects—another piece in the pattern that is compiling circumstantial evidence beyond a reasonable doubt that the UFO's exist and are probably piloted by super-minded beings from some mighty center of galactic civilization that pities us for thinking we are that center.

We might as well get prepared for it—in case.

CHAPTER 7

Stricken Sighters

November 4, 1957, Itaipu Fort, Brazil, 2:03
A.M. (from *The Reference For Outstanding UFO
Sighting Reports.*)

It was a quiet, moonless tropical night, and the
army garrison at Itaipu was peacefully asleep, two
sentries at the top of the fortification going about
routine tasks in a relaxed manner.

A new "star" suddenly burst into brilliant life
among others in the cloudless sky over the Atlantic. The sentries watched in detached interest until
they realized it was not a star but a luminous
flying object coming straight toward the fort. . . .

It hovered about 120 to 180 feet above the
highest turret and then was motionless. The weird
object was large, about the size of a big Douglas,
but disc-shaped and encircled by an eerie orange
glow. . . .

The two men heard a distinct humming
sound . . . then the nightmare. Something hot
touched their faces. . . . An intolerable wave of
heat struck the two soldiers. . . .

One sentry staggered, his only conscious purpose to escape from that invisible fire that seemed
to be burning him alive. . . . He blacked out and
fell to the ground.

The other sentry had the horrible feeling that
his clothes were on fire. He began to scream
desperately, stumbling and crying like a trapped
animal. . . . His loud cries awoke the garrison.
Inside the installation everything was confusion. . . .

After the UFO left, it was found that both sentries were badly burned. . . . Both had first-de-
gree and deep second-degree burns on more than
10% of the body. . . . The sentry who could
talk later was in deep nervous shock. . . . The
nightmare had lasted three minutes.

This account, corroborated by all the men at the fort and checked out by UFO investigators, is the single most dramatic instance of *physiological EM effects* caused by UFO's on the human body.

It is not known whether that UFO deliberately aimed some sort of "heat ray" at the two men or not. At any rate, the fort was not harmed, and all electrical circuits (which had been knocked out) went back on after the saucer left.

This strange kind of "invisible burning" of the skin has been reported many times, giving us another strong pattern that cannot be refuted and which attests to the reality of the UFO's, even if we haven't the least idea why such burn effects should occur.

To make it clear, this book is not going to *solve* the mystery of the UFO's but merely tabulate all the *patterns* exhibited by the saucers that prove them to be real and not to be ignored by the government and the scientific establishment as "unimportant" or "illusionary" phenomena.

It was very important and hardly an illusion to the two Brazilian sentries and to many other terrified people who have felt those eerie EM effects of the UFO's. Following are a few more choice examples of the "burn-ray" effect:

——November 6, 1957, near Mirom, Indiana. Rene Gilham saw an intensely bright UFO hovering over his farm, and the next day his face began to itch and burn, building up to where he was hospitalized for 11 days before his swollen, reddened skin became normal.

——May 5, 1958, near San Carlos, Uruguay. Encountering a dazzling bright UFO, a pilot felt such intense heat in his cockpit that he was forced to remove some clothing.

——July 1, 1954, Griffis AFB, New York. Two pilots sent up to intercept a UFO felt heat "like the blast of a blowtorch in the face," and when their cockpit became a "hellhole," they bailed out, and their plane crashed.

Imagination? Hardly, when two seasoned pilots abandoned their jet over a populated area, well knowing the possible results—which unfortunately happened. Their plane crashed in a town, killing several people. Sticking to their story, the pilots were not court-martialed—obviously because the Air Force knew they had *really* encountered something strange and menacing from a UFO.

Other EM Bio-Effects

The "burn-ray" is only one of the physiological effects experienced by various UFO observers. Certain other EM effects have been reported, including temporary "paralysis," as in the following accounts: (From *"The Reference."*)

——September 10, 1954, Quarouble, France (partly quoted from before). Marius DeWilde saw a dark shape on a railroad track, from which emerged two small creatures in "diving suits." Then, he says, "I was no more than six feet from the two forms when I was blinded by an extremely powerful light, like a magnesium flare. . . . I closed my eyes and tried to yell, but I couldn't. It was just as if I had been paralyzed. I tried to move but my legs wouldn't obey me. . . . Finally the beam of light went out. I then recovered the use of my muscles and ran. . . ."

——September 17, 1954, Cenon (Vienne), France. M. Yves David was bicycling on a dark night when he felt a strange sensation of discomfort—a sort of prickling or itching all over his body. "Just as if I had had an electric shock," he described it. The disagreeable prickling sensation did not stop, and before long he was paralyzed. It was then he noticed the dark object parked in the road ahead. From it came a small creature who touched him on the shoulder and uttered a sound that was inhuman and incomprehensible, after which he returned to his UFO craft and sped away. At the same time, M. David recovered the use of his limbs.

——October 16, 1954, southeast of Dieppe, France. Dr. Henri Robert was driving when he spied four discs flying in formation in the sky. One of them "peeled off" and came swooping low over his car. Dr. Robert says he felt a kind of "electric shock," and at the same time his engine died and his headlights went out. Dr. Robert then became paralyzed and could not move as the UFO landed on the road and a little creature 3 feet tall shone a light at him. When the tiny man and the UFO left moments later, Dr. Robert was able to move and start his car.

The similarity of these three accounts is striking, all occurring in France in 1954, when an intense "wave" of UFO's appeared all over the nation for weeks. It was also the first time, except for sporadic reports around the world, that the "little men" seemed to appear all over and many UFO's landed or flew low at treetop level.

The many UFO landers and the tiny men reported throughout France by people who had never heard of anyone else's experience cannot be laid down to vivid imagination or "copycat" reports vying for sensationalism.

Both Dr. Jacques Vallee (author of *Anatomy of a Phenomenon* and *Challenge To Science: The UFO's*) and Aimé Michel (author of three saucer books) interviewed many of these French observers and collected affidavits attesting to their reliable character. Furthermore, their stories never varied, and they were genuinely frightened as they talked and relived their experiences.

This represents another kind of *pattern* relating to UFO's—how their operations change from year to year, sometimes being mainly high-up flights, then low-level missions, then a rash of landings with little men stepping out, etc. More on this later.

More "Human Effects"

The variety of physical effects that are felt or experienced by UFO sighters can be seen in the following encounters with saucers:

——November 10, 1957, Madison, Ohio. Mrs. Leita Kuhn saw a huge object as big as a house, shaped like an acorn, over her garage. She stared as if in a trance for a half hour at the dazzling bright object, her eyes hurting. A few days later a body rash developed, plus some failing of the vision. Her doctor said her eyes looked as though they had suffered radiation burns, but it later proved that there was no permanent damage. The rash on her arms and legs might be from shock at what she had seen, the doctor suggested, but he could not be sure.

——February 20, 1958, near Espanola, New Mexico. The witness suffered skin burns with reported radioactivity present upon encountering a landed UFO.

——August 6, 1955, Cincinnati, Ohio. The witness had badly irritated eyes after staring at a brilliant UFO.

——September 28, 1954, Bouzais, France. The witness was first paralyzed, then lost consciousness, when spying a nearby UFO.

Admittedly, some of these "EM effects" could be sheer fright from a traumatic experience. But the many hundreds of cases reporting a "prickling sensation" or "electric shock" or "paralyzed legs" cannot all be placed in this convenient psychosomatic pigeonhole.

When one is panic-stricken or terrorized, adrenalin shooting into his bloodstream gives him the power to *flee* in almost all cases. We all know how fear "lends wings" to our feet. For a person to be terrified and remain rooted to the spot is somewhat of a contradiction of known human reactions except in comparatively rare cases.

Therefore, the overly large proportion of paralysis cases, when confronted by a UFO or its occupants, is another pattern of saucer data tending to back up their reality rather than disprove it.

As for the repeated appearance of "little men" or creatures 3 or 4 feet high, it was not only in 1954 in France that they were reported. There is a significant worldwide pattern after 1954, which will be taken up later, but notice that none of them were called "little *green* men," as the popular jokes on the subject, invented by the publicity paranoids, would have us believe.

Animal EM Effects

UFO's have also affected other living things besides people in various ways. One of the most universally reported side effects of the appearance of a UFO is the way nearby domestic animals are affected—dogs howling dismally, horses bolting, cows showing fear and restricting their milk output, even bulls ripping loose from stakes and chains.

In many cases people were warned in advance that something unusual must be around by the peculiar behavior of their pets. Later they saw the UFO's that had caused this animal alarm.

This is also an EM effect, since it is well-known that dogs and other animals can hear sounds beyond the human range and thus may first detect the peculiar whine or pulsating hum that is often heard from UFO's at close range.

But why should the animals, who have heard many other kinds of whining sounds from earthly machines, react in such instinctive *fear*? This again is a point that should give biological scientists pause before they dismiss the UFO's as "nonsense." Animals cannot talk, but their howls speak louder than words, and nobody can accuse animals of being deliberate liars or mass hallucinators.

This animal reaction to the presence of UFO's is therefore another valid affirmative item in the circumstantial evidence offered in the saucer controversy. All these parts of the great "pattern" will be summarized at the end of this book to see how much acceptable evidence has piled up in favor of UFO's being fact rather than fiction.

EM Enigma

The EM effects in the vegetable kingdom include the following:

Trees turning black.

Tree branches dried and curling.

Trees "carbonized" as if petrified (turned to stone).

Grayish stain on greenery.

Grass scorched.

Shrubbery set on fire.

Radioactivity level higher in patches of vegetation.

But little research has been done in this area, and information is sparse, leading to no useful conclusions or surmises.

A strange new pattern also comes out of the EM effects, as pointed out by the late Professor Maney, mentioned before. Checking all cases, Dr. Maney was surprised to notice that only eight EM cases were on record prior to the sudden rash of sightings with EM effects that came from France in 1954. Since then EM cases have increased in all countries.

One possible answer to this oddity is that worldwide press coverage of UFO phenomena was very poor up to about 1952, and the most "lurid" cases involving burn-rays and such were probably instantly consigned to the wastebasket as being fabricated fantasies. Continual research by UFOlogists in old newspaper files may resolve this point as more and more old, forgotten UFO sightings are dug up.

On the other hand, it may be part of the UFO series of "patterns." Landing and low-flying UFO's also tended to be rare prior to 1952, and most EM cases are contingent on close approach of the saucer. Or it may even be that the saucerians deliberately began using EM phenomena, if we assume that these are apart from their power plants and are controllable forces.

Further speculation of course is useless. But in explaining away the EM effects, the anti-UFO authorities have not been too successful.

They suggested, first, that all EM effects could coincide with major disturbances on the sun, which are known to deluge earth with protons and electrons and sometimes black out radio around the world for hours.

But when Professor Maney charted "rashes" of EM reports and compared them with the known solar outbreaks, there was no slightest correlation. Scratch one "scientific" explanation.

All other natural manifestations—the auroras, electrical storms, upper-air ionization factors—never coincided by the calendar with outbreaks of EM sightings. The increase in EM cases simply followed increases and waves of UFO sightings, nothing else.

In summary, the high abundance (33 percent) of EM effects of all kinds in the reports of landing or low-flying UFO's is another part of the pattern of proof that seems to be slowly but overwhelmingly deciding that the flying saucers are not myths but machines.

CHAPTER 8

Unearthly Phenomena

November 4, 1954, near Pontal, Brazil. Jose Alves of Pontal was fishing in the Pardo River near Pontal. The area was deserted, the night quiet, with only a slight breeze blowing from the east. Suddenly Alves spotted a strange object in the sky, apparently heading toward him.

He watched, transfixed, as it closed in with a wobbling motion and landed. It was so near he could have touched it, he said.

The object—appearing as two washbowls placed together—was about 10 to 15 feet in diameter. He was too frightened to run. Three little men, clad in white clothing with close-fitting skull caps, emerged from a windowlike opening in the side of the small object.

Their skin appeared to be quite dark. Alves stood terror-stricken. Then, as suddenly as they had come, they jumped back into their machine, which took off vertically as swiftly and silently as it had come. (From *"The Reference."*))

As with several previous reports of sightings, this encounter with a UFO produced *terror* in the witness. There are many other cases where the observers unashamedly admit being afraid upon seeing a strange machine, even if it doesn't land and no creatures come out.

The Terrifying Unknowns

These terrified reactions are also numerous enough to make a pattern—a pattern of *fear of the unknown*—which in itself is another bit of circumstantial evidence that the UFO's exist and are *alien* to earth. Whatever the saucers are and whatever the beings are in them, they seem capable of striking instinctive and involuntary dread in human observers.

It is almost as if at first glance the witness *knows* they are weird craft and nonhuman creatures from another world. The following sightings will give this premise more solid support:

———October 30, 1957, Casper, Wyoming. A young couple, Shirly Moyer and Hugh Pulju, were driving ten miles north of Casper when a round, shiny object appeared in the road about 250 feet ahead of their car.

"It was as big as a house and had two pointed peaks on it," Miss Moyer said afterwards. "It glowed about halfway up. I've been scared before, but that thing had me petrified . . ."

———June 22, 1966, along Lake Erie. Evelyn Wolff relates this experience: "A friend and I were sitting on a big rock on Lake Erie . . . looking at the stars. . . . Far far away we saw what looked like a star except it was so very red. All at once it started to fall, (then) darted back up, hovered in one place, then darted to the right, stayed there a few seconds, then darted left. . . . It kind of frightened me, as I never saw a star misbehave before."

———At the end of one 1954 sighting in France involving small men who stepped out of a landed saucer, the report says: "Madame LeBoueuf was found in a state of nervous collapse. She was put to bed, where she remained for two days with a high fever. As for the dog, it was still trembling with fright three days later."

———In Salvador on February 24, 1958, a lawyer and a friend were driving between Nazare and Salvador City when a large, luminous object came down. They stopped to step out and look and were horrified to see it come closer and hover over them. The frightened driver sprang back into the car.

———Again in Brazil, in 1958, a party of young people out driving came upon a UFO. Goncalves, one of the group, said his "hair stood on end."

———In Giwa, New Guinea in June 1959, a trader spied a UFO that came down and hovered 500 feet high. "I was very frightened," he later said, "But I couldn't take my eyes off it. . . ."

——August 12, 1953, near Rapid City, South Dakota. When an Air Force pilot was sent to check a UFO, he admitted being "scared" and even asked if he could break off the intercept.

——July 26, 1952, Washington, D.C. Air Force interceptors were sent up to investigate four or more fast-moving "blips" seen by radar. One, Lt. William Patterson, was badly frightened when a group of glowing objects surrounded his plane. As the CAA radar operators below watched the blips on the scope cluster around his plane, the pilot asked them in a scared voice what he should do. There was a stunned silence; no one answered. . . .

——November 3, 1957, near Levelland, Texas. Early on that date Sheriff Weir Clem suddenly found himself thrown into . . . a rapid series of nightmarish reports. . . . A phone call (came) from a "terrified" farmhand who had seen a huge torpedo-shaped UFO swoop over his truck. . . . Jim Wheeler reported a large egg-shaped "thing" parked on a road. . . . Altogether there were 14 calls from panicky people who had encountered UFO's at close range.

In a certain number of cases people seeing strange UFO's hovering nearby or meeting "little men" from landed saucers have had extreme nervous reactions, often requiring medical care.

In several cases police officers who reported UFO's and stuck to their stories eventually met so much ridicule, plus the frowns of their superiors, that they resigned from the force. In at least one case a police officer was so haunted by what he had seen that his behavior resulted in divorce from his wife, and today he lives a hermitlike existence, shunning people and wishing he "had never seen that crazy thing."

Uncanny Flying Objects

Fear, however, is not as generally expressed by UFO sighters as a sense of the uncanny. This is almost universal in the reports and indicates a definite feeling among

the observers that they have seen an other-worldly phenomenon. Note the following expressions used in connection with sightings:

——November 14, 1956, near Mobile, Alabama.
An airlines pilot, Captain Hull, upon seeing a zigzagging object during flight along with his copilot, said:
"MacIntosh and I sat there completely flabbergasted at
this unnerving exhibition. . . ."

——September 8, 1958, SAC headquarters. Upon
sighting a hovering UFO, one officer among others stated: "We watched in awe for several minutes."

——August 3, 1951, Silver Lake, Michigan. Walter
N. Webb, astronomer, saw a yellow light making peculiar motions in the sky and averred later: "I had seen
something strange in the sky that I could not explain.
No known object (on earth) I could think of followed
a path like that."

——March 16, 1961, aboard an icebreaker near
Antartica. Rubens J. Villela, an experienced Moon-
watch (satellite) observer, spied a luminous teardrop
whose appearance was "out of this world. I can think
of nothing on earth which would reproduce the phenomenon."

——June 30, 1954, over the North Atlantic south
of Goose Bay, Labrador. A BOAC pilot, Captain
Howard, upon seeing a "blob" UFO pacing the plane
for 18 minutes, called it the "strangest eighty-five-mile
journey in my life. . . . Maneuverable and controlled
intelligently. . . . It must have been some weird form
of spaceship from another world."

——August 1, 1952, Cincinnati, Ohio. George F.
Kyle, fire inspector at a GE plant, saw an oval shape
as big as the moon and said it was "hard to believe and
was like a dream."

——Winter 1952, near Stockholm, Sweden. A farm
couple saw a disc that seemed on fire yet abruptly
faded out of view, and the woman said their skin
pricked and "got goose pimples" at the eerie appari-
tion.

Angel Hair

The pattern of unearthly phenomena connected with UFO's goes in other directions besides human reactions. One of the oddest mysteries is the so-called "angel hair" seemingly dropped at times by saucers flying overhead, as mentioned briefly before.

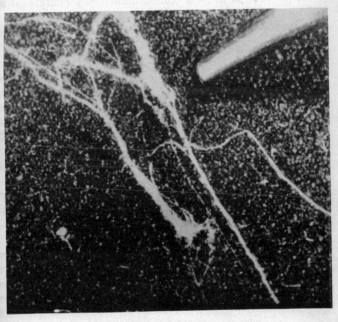

Angel hair as seen under a microscope.

But there are many more cases from all over the world through the past 20 years, again bearing the stamp of a repeated reality. The angel hair had often been touched and even gathered for later analysis, but it always "evaporated" or otherwise disintegrated swiftly before reaching a laboratory.

Incidentally, in both the French sightings at Oloron and Gaillac of the same cigar-shaped mother ship, fluffy angel hair was reported to have drifted down, and "for several hours clumps of it hung in the trees, on the telephone wires, and on the roofs of the houses."

A more detailed account of this UFO "discharge" is as follows:

November 16, 1953, Reseda, California, sighting by Mrs. Louis Dangelo. In her own words:

"We were watching three jet planes. Then, behind them, we saw a huge silvery ball . . . it moved up and down and even sideways. Finally, a long streamer of white stuff, almost like a vapor trail, spewed out of its back end.

"It detached itself from the ball and began settling earthward. It spread out, stringy sort of, like white wool being shredded, and it dropped down all over the neighborhood like cobwebs. . . ."

The term "cobweb" is often used by those witnessing this queer white material exuded by UFO's. The anti-UFO critics seized upon this to "explain" all such angel hair as the well-known migration of newly hatched tiny spiders, who spin out cobwebby fluff and ride it in the wind like "balloonists."

However, no entomologist has yet explained how this can occur in the winter, too, since the spiders migrate only in the spring and the fall. It seems almost stupid for scientists to offer such explanations that are so patently erroneous.

From the list of 17 cases compiled by Professor Charles Maney, the following reports speak for themselves:

——May 30, 1953, Palmerston, New Zealand. "Four round objects glistening in the sun threw off some kind of whitish substance . . . a white silky strip about twelve feet long settled on a tree."

——October 13, 1953, Pleasant Hill, California. "The ball was about three times the size of a full moon. . . . Suddenly a stream of white lacy substance flowed from the ball."

——November 16, 1953, San Fernando, California. "After ten or fifteen seconds the object . . . emitted some shining cobweblike substance which began to drift to earth."

———October 22, 1954, Marysville, Ohio. "Fifteen thousand spectators at a football match watched a flight of saucers which dropped candy-floss type streamers."

The entomologists might have difficulty denying that 5,000 witnesses saw that flight of UFO's drop down ngel hair.

Professor Maney also gathered quotes from various itnesses, describing the strange properties of the cobweby strands:

———"When rolled up into a ball, they rapidly became gelatinous, then sublimed in the air and disappeared."

———"Quickly disintegrated when handled."

———"Held between the fingers, it dissolves into nothing."

ading Saucers

Another uncanny set of phenomena displayed by many JFO's, according to eyewitnesses, is the peculiar ways aucers will appear or disappear, falling in the following ategories:

—Saucers that just fade from sight without growing maller or receding in the distance.

—Bright saucers seen at night that suddenly "blink ut."

—Saucers that have "fuzzy" outlines.

—Saucers that appear in a misty "cloud" of their own nd usually "dissolve" into a cloud again.

—Saucers that seem to dive straight to the ground, eaving no wreckage, at least none officially admitted.

All of these may be lumped together as indicating that JFO's can do "tricks" that no machine or object on earth ver can. One theory is that the UFO's do not speed hrough the huge gulfs of space, from their home world to arth, but enter a "dimension door" and appear in the wink of an eye.

Yes, this is the old science fiction "gimmick" of the

convenient "space warp," which allows the author to whisl
his space hero anywhere in short order and thus not dela
the story's action.

UFO truth may be stranger than fiction—the sauce
rians may have made this earthly "plot device" com
true.

Certainly this would make it much more reasonabl
and understandable that so many saucers are constantl
flitting around earth, perhaps coming originally from
star system unthinkable light-years away. If they can sim
ply "fade into" earth's skies, then "fade home" again i
mere seconds, one of the major arguments against the ex
istence of UFO's would be eliminated—that the sauce
rians from any star more than 30 light-years away woul
spend an entire lifetime, if equal to ours, just going bac
and forth once.

The UFOnauts may utilize tremendous secrets of spac
and time we know nothing about that make travel throug
the universe fantastically easy. Who knows?

Paranormal Pattern

In his book, *Challenge to Science: The UFO Enigma*
Dr. Jacques Vallee, astrophysicist and mathematician
states that "The boundaries of the unbelievable have beer
reached, both by accounts describing experiences an
phenomena that seem without precedent in scientific histo
ry and by explanations, that if taken seriously, would cal
for a *complete overthrow of current scientific concepts.*"
(Italics supplied.)

At any rate, the puzzling ways in which saucers car
abruptly appear or vanish is another part of the *patterr
of unearthliness* surrounding the mysterious UFO's
Human hallucinations, fed by imagination, could hardly
devise such eerie characteristics, which adds another
brick to the circumstantial evidence building up for the
existence of genuine UFO's from some other realm be
yond earth.

CHAPTER 9

The Endless Waves

"The temporary lull in reporting (UFO's) that Project Blue Book had experienced in early July (1952) proved to be only the calm before the storm. By mid-July we were getting about 20 reports a day plus frantic calls from intelligence officers all over the U.S., as every Air Force installation in the U.S. was being swamped with reports. . . ."

THESE WORDS OF Captain Edward J. Ruppelt, in his book *The Report on Unidentified Flying Objects,* are perhaps the best expression of what a "UFO wave" is.

Far from appearing uniformly around earth throughout the years, the saucers have very definitely concentrated in certain specific regions at various times. Every portion of earth has had its "wave," namely, a major jump in sightings for weeks or even months, as the following chart of NICAP indicates:

FLAPS (Based on U.S. publicity)	CONCEN- TRATIONS	YEAR	PERIOD	MAIN LOCATIONS
X		1947	June-July	Western United States
	X	1950	First Half	Midwest, West, & SW U.S.
X		1952	July-August	Eastern United States
	X	1952	Sept.-October	Europe
	X	1954	April-December	World-Wide
	X	1954	October	France
	X	1955	August	Midwest United States
X		1957	November	Midwest, Southwest U.S., South America
	X	1959	June-August	Pacific Ocean, Australia, New Guinea, New Zealand
	X	1960	August	Northern California
	X	1962	May, July-August	Argentina
	X	1962	September	New Jersey

The "flaps" refer to times when the press gave saucers a big play out of proportion to the actual number of sightings, which did not constitute a real wave. "Concentrations," on the other hand, indicate a true big wave of UFO's for that region.

However, others disagree with NICAP's listing and call the 1952 "flap" a true worldwide wave instead. Other insights and changes may come about when further tabulations show the true figures for each year on an earthwide basis.

The flap of 1947 was touched off, of course, by Kenneth Arnold's famed sighting of nine disks, and the American press headlined almost every new saucer for weeks and months before the furor finally subsided.

The 1952 flap was the occasion of the so-called "attack on Washington," when some 67 UFO's were seen or spotted by radar, all of them concentrating in and around the capital of the U.S. There was, of course, no actual attack and no shooting by the saucers, which merely seemed to be "scouting" the city and outflying all the jets sent to intercept or chase them away.

As for the 1957 flap, many UFOlogists would again disagree with NICAP and call it a true wave, at least for South America. In America the flap came about when the launching of Sputnik II by Russia triggered off a rash of sightings here, some of them genuine but most of them probably out of hysteria.

Regarding the waves, note that 1954 saw world wide sightings on an unprecedented scale, with the peaks of UFO observations in the U.S., South America, and Europe (particularly France).

Champion Wave

But the greatest worldwide wave, not shown on NICAP's chart, started off in the summer of 1965 and continued almost unabated into the spring of 1966. In America the press went wild as region after region reported UFO's by the dozens and the hundreds.

First Oklahoma and surrounding states in mid-1965 reported a wave of saucers, including one amazing "fleet" of hundreds of UFO's. Then in the fall of 1965, New Jersey kept the wires humming with the notorious Wanaque Dam sightings, which continued well into 1966.

At almost the same time in late 1965, the saucers invaded New Hampshire, out of which came the recent book by John Fuller, *Incident at Exeter*.

In the spring of 1966 the scene shifted to Michigan, around Ann Arbor, where many college girls reported saucers. It was here that the notorious "swamp gas" explanation of Dr. J. Allen Hynek came forth in behalf of the Air Force. However, Dr. Hynek was actually misquoted, claiming that only two saucer sightings could be so

An Australian sheep rancher, W. C. Hall, took this photo in 1954. Considered authentic.

explained, and candidly admitted that the others seemed to be genuine unknowns.

While the U.S. had this rash of sightings from coast to coast, an even bigger wave of saucers was reported all over South America, much of it ignored by our American press, as so often happens with foreign sightings.

Successive or concurrent waves of UFO's during 1965 and 1966 were also reported from Europe, Asia, Japan, Africa, and Australia. Even the "saucer curtain" that had suppressed UFO sightings behind the Iron Curtain was breached as reports filtered through from Russia, Poland, Czechoslovakia and elsewhere in eastern Europe.

Up until 1966 the Soviet Union had made official announcements that the UFO's were all illusions and were not seen by their people—an obvious untruth. Then, in April of 1967, the Russians made an about-face and not only admitted widespread UFO sightings in the Soviet Union but also claimed to have tracked them by radar for the past 20 years. And they, too, have begun to set their scientists to work on the mystery of the elusive saucers.

Pre-1947 Waves

NICAP's list can also be extended into the past, for saucer sightings did not begin in 1947 but long before that, perhaps thousands of years ago or at least several centuries ago.

Dr. Jacques Vallee, in *UFO's: Anatomy of a Phenomenon,* lists waves in various parts of the world for the years 1881, 1885, 1905, and 1913. Oddly, reports were low during the years from 1914 to 1946 for unknown reasons. The saucers showed up only sporadically.

Then 1946 again saw a wave, this time mainly in Sweden where hundreds of "ghost rockets" were reported flying over their land. They were first thought to be Russian test missiles, similar to the German V-2's during the war, but it was soon discovered that Russia had no such rockets, nor had any other country on earth. Thus, these torpedo-shaped apparitions are now recognized as a UFO wave.

World War II fighter planes being paced by "foo-fighters."

One other wave of peculiar flying objects preceded the Swedish ghost rockets. During the war, in 1944 and 1945, the queer "foo fighters" appeared, pacing Allied bombers and giving our airmen a scare at the thought they might be a new "secret weapon" of the Nazis. However, we learned after the war that the Germans thought it was a device of *ours*.

The foo-fighter UFO's were all small, glowing balls, some only inches wide, others perhaps a yard or two. Silently and enigmatically they flew alongside planes for a while, then vanished, leaving the riddle hanging in the air to this day.

Ancient UFO's

Have flying saucers been visiting earth for thousands of years? Evidence is piling up, from researches into old documents and rocords, that such is actually the case. (*The*

Flying Saucer Story by Brinsley le Poer Trench.)

Back in Biblical times Ezekiel the prophet may well have recorded one of the earliest UFO's:

"And I looked and behold, a whirlwind came out of the north, a great cloud, and a fire unfolding itself . . . as the color of burnished brass . . . and their appearance and their work was as it were a wheel within a wheel."

Just as "technical" sounding is an excerpt from the Annals of Thutmose III of Egypt, back around 1500 B.C.:

". . . it was a circle of fire that was coming in the sky. . . These things became more numerous in the sky (and) shone more . . . than the brightness of the sun."

In Roman times many references were made to queer objects in the sky, similar to this report from 218 B.C.:

"At Arpi (was) a shield in the sky . . . during the night two moons were seen. Phantom ships appeared in the sky."

During the reign of Charlemagne, A.D. 742 to 814, the Comte de Gabalis wrote:

"One day, among other instances, it chanced at Lyons that three men and a woman were seen descending from these aerial ships."

Other brief quotes through the centuries sound remarkably similar to present-day flying saucer reports:

A.D. 1254—"A kind of large ship (in the sky)."

A.D. 1290—Monks in Yorkshire were excited to see a "large round silver disk" flying slowly overhead.

A.D. 1320—After the death of an abbot, a "great light" appeared in the sky and "moved from one place to another."

A.D. 1520—In Prussia a great "burning beam" landed, then took off into the sky again.

A.D. 1619—The Swiss saw a long, bright object flying along a lake.

A.D. 1686—A German astronomer observed "a burning glob (that) remained immovable (hovered) for one-eighth of an hour."

A.D. 1718—"A great light that suddenly appeared in the western sky. . . . It moved more slowly than a falling star in a direct line. . . . (it was) pear-shaped."

A.D. 1741—"A ball of fire . . . oval in shape."

A.D. 1762—A huge spindle-shaped object was seen crossing the face of the sun at two observatories.

A.D. 1777—Charles Messier, famed French astronomer, saw a dark, round object in space near earth.

19th-Century Saucers

From 1800 on, the sightings are more numerous. At least 200 reliable 19-century reports are known, of which the following is the most remarkable and best documented, being seen by uncounted thousands of people and written up in detail in dozens of newspapers:

————November 22, 1896. A "cigar-shaped object with stubby wings" sailed slowly over San Francisco and environs, seen by thousands of people. In the following year the same strange zeppelinlike craft—but before the zeppelin was invented—was observed over Omaha, Kansas City, and Chicago as it crisscrossed over the U.S. Total witnesses must have been in the millions, all describing it in approximately the same way. It was estimated to be 200 feet long, 30 feet in diameter, and had rows of green lights on its sides.

This "cigar" craft is still an unsolved mystery today and very definitely rates as a UFO.

From 1900 to 1946 over one hundred "good" UFO reports have been unearthed by researchers going through old newspaper files. They weren't called UFO's in those days, or flying saucers, but by their descriptions there is no mistaking the fact that they are the same type of unknowns we see in today's sky:

1904—A ship at sea sighted three luminous disks that climbed into a cloud bank at high speed.

1909, July to September—Hundreds of people in New Zealand saw a strange "airship" in the sky.

1917—This is one of the most celebrated cases. On October 13 an "immense globe" like an "aeroplane of light" was seen by 70,000 people of Fatima, Portugal. The UFO did a "fantastic dance" in the sky and rotated with the greatest speed, also shedding down angel-hair "snowflakes."

1926—Another conspicious case, wherein a well-known explorer in Mongolia, with trekking party, caught sight of a huge oval-shaped object with a shiny surface, flying at unbelievable speed.

1935—During the Ethiopian War a disc hovered over Addis Ababa, seen by many eyes.

1942—During the war a large aluminum disc zoomed straight down at a cruiser of the Netherlands Navy, then veered upward and circled the Dutch ship for more than three hours.

1944—The foo fighters were first seen and kept appearing to the end of the war the next year.

1946 (before Arnold)—Captain Jack Puckett and his crew, flying a C-47, saw a cigar-shaped object flash past them at terrific speed.

After the war, throughout 1946 and up to mid-1947, about a dozen UFO reports had been made already in America, but none of them caught fire as did Kenneth Arnold's report of June 24, 1947.

Modern Waves

And then the flying saucer "craze" was on, resulting in an average of some 550 Air Force cases per year, with a peak of 1,501 reports in 1952 followed by 1,060 for 1966, the next highest year.

Professor Charles Maney has compiled a list of a different series of waves, which is intriguing in context with the numerical waves. He points out that the *types* of UFO's have changed periodically, in a fairly distinct manner, as follows:

—During 1944–45 only the *foo fighters* were seen.

—In 1946 the *ghost rockets* of Sweden appeared.

—In 1947 the *discs* began to appear in enormous numbers.

—Around 1950 the huge *cigars* began to come into prominence.

—In 1951 a series of baffling *green fireballs,* which were not meteors, blazed across the skies of New Mexico over our missiles ranges and atomic installations.

—From 1952 to 1955 *angel hair* falling from UFO's was first reported widely.

—1954 in France particularly the "little men" were widely seen.

—1957 saw the uprise of many *electromagnetic effects*.

His list stops there, but we can add more now:

—1960 to date, many more saucers make landings on earth.

—1964 on, a big increase in the number of low-flying, or "treetop," UFO's.

—1965–1966 on, there is a big increase in the number of UFO's doing high speed maneuvers in the sky.

Certain UFO researchers, notably Donald Keyhoe of NICAP, have speculated that just as earthly models of cars or planes change and improve each year, so do the UFO "models." Another concept is that the above pattern is a systematic exploration and study of earth and its civilization. More on that in another chapter.

Wave Pattern

The series of saucer-sighting waves constitutes another pattern that adds to the circumstantial evidence that UFO's are real, not illusionary; otherwise they would appear in the *random* pattern. The mere bunching up of UFO's and the geographical shift of the waves, plus (as Maney noted) a change of models, all add heavy weight to the probability that UFO's are intelligently made and controlled.

The wave of 1965–66, the biggest of them all, has had its impact on the authorities, particularly Secretary-General U Thant of the U.N., who during 1966 conferred in private with Dr. J. Allen Hynek, John Fuller (UFO author), and Gordon Evans, well-known civilian UFOlogist. The result may be the formation of some kind of U.N. "committee on UFO's" to study them on an international basis, since the saucers are a global phenomenon and therefore can affect all people on earth.

Wave after wave of UFO's—why? And have saucers seemingly been visiting earth for ages? No one knows or even suspects the answers.

CHAPTER 10

The UFOnauts

"I have been reading your UFO accounts (referring to the author's syndicated picture panel, OUR SPACE AGE) . . . I've experienced same.

"Firstly, I'm 45 years old, a Christian, anti-alcohol, an electronics engineer. I don't believe in spooks, ghosts, haunted houses, etc.

"In the spring of 1960 I was living in northern New York (state). One warm evening after supper I decided to go fish bullheads. . . . I had to drive about 4 miles, where I left my car and had to walk about one-half mile through a woods to a creek where I have fished many, many times.

"The fishing was good . . . darkness had set in . . . started for my car . . . when I heard a high-pitched hum. I could see this object coming downstream, low over the water . . . and land(ing) . . . it settled down very slowly to the ground. A light on its top turned around, something like radar (antennas). Now this you won't believe.

"But two small creatures left the object and dragged what might be a fireman's hose to the water. One of them went back in the machine while the other one splashed his hands in the water like a small child might play.

"The creature came out of the machine and the two of them seemed to enjoy our light gravity by the way they jumped around. Light of various colors came from each creature. I have thought about it since and I believe that light of various shades of intensity is their method of thought transmission . . .

"I watched them from behind the tree until it (the saucer) left. It seemed they were after water. But (with) all these years of physics and electronics (I've had) and I've never seen the likes of it.

"I've only told 2 or 3 people about it as people are doubtful of such tales. Some day we'll know."

—Anonymous
Syracuse, N.Y.

THIS MAN GAVE me no name or return address, obviously wanting to avoid publicity. And it is now thought, among UFO investigators, that it is not necessarily true that the landings of small-sized humanoids *began* around 1952, when such reports increased rapidly in numbers.

It may very well be that all early UFO sighting reports from 1947 to 1952, were automatically thrown away by the Air Force as being too "unbelievable" when any mention of "little men" was made.

Also, witnesses of small UFOnauts prior to 1952 were undoubtedly afraid to breathe the story to a soul for fear of being instantly classed as "lunatic." Therefore, it may be that many saucer landings and the appearance of their operators are lost forever to UFOlogy.

Nevertheless, there are early recorded sightings of "small humanoids" who stepped out of parked saucers, particularly in Sweden during the ghost-rocket wave of 1946. Some reports dug up by UFO researchers go back to 1897, when the strange "airship" toured over a startled America, as related before. The huge UFO was seen to land and disgorge "tiny men," at one place.

The Little Men

But it was not until 1952 that reports began pyramiding about UFOnauts' emerging from landed saucers— once again to form a *pattern,* for by far the majority of them mentioned *little* men.

Their sizes, as estimated by various observers, range from 18 inches to 4 or 5 feet tall, but a figure around 3 feet tall is most common.

Brinsley le Poer Trench adds up over 2,000 cases of saucer landings since 1947. His figure is probably far from the true number, since any estimator has available

to him only a limited number of sighting reports, such as
from the Air Force, from NICAP, and from newspaper
files. No comprehensive "UFO sighting guide" has yet
been compiled by anyone, hence it is difficult to extract
correct totals of any phase of UFO data, from 1947 to
date.

But the little men who ride UFO's seem established beyond any reasonable doubt by existent accounts, of which
the following are typical samples:

——July 2, 1950, Ontario, Canada. A man and his
wife saw a UFO land in a river (sic), and 10 tiny humanoids emerged, each about 3 feet 6 inches tall.

——October 9, 1954, Rinkerode, Germany. A man
saw a small, cigar-shaped object that had landed near a
road, from which came four "little creatures" who
worked on the underside of their craft, as if making re-
pairs. They were about 1.20 meters (4 feet) tall.

——October 12, 1954, Teheran, Iran. When a disc-
UFO swooped low over a crowd, one of the witnesses
spied the UFOnaut within, whom he described as
"small and dressed in black."

——October 12, 1954 (again), Mamora Forest, Mor-
occo. A French engineer observed a small being, about
4 feet tall, enter a saucer that quickly took off.

——October 17, 1954, Isle of Capri. An artist taking
a walk came upon a landed saucer that was 16 feet in
diameter, out of which came four little beings dressed
in coveralls.

But sometimes, instead of little men, they are "little
women," as in the next account:

—October 15, 1957, near São Francisco do Sul, Brazil. A farmer describes the four small occupants of a
saucer as small men 5 feet 4 inches tall, while the fifth
was a girl 4 feet 8 inches tall . . . fair-skinned and
freckled, with high cheekbones, pointed chin, and vivid
blue "Chinese-type" (slanted) eyes.

1954 Humanoids

Jacques Vallee, in *The Humanoids* (published by

Flying Saucer Review, England), lists 200 cases of landing or low-flying UFO's in 1954 alone, most of them in France, where such reports were freely made and written up in newspapers:

———September 10, 1954, Quarouble, France. The witness first came upon a UFO that landed on railroad tracks, then encountered creatures "such as I had never seen before. . . . The beam of my (flash) light caught a reflection of glass or metal where his face should have been. I had the distinct impression that his head was enclosed in a diver's helmet . . . They were very short, probably less than three and a half feet tall."

An Italian engineer, Gianpietro Monguzzi, took a series of photos of a saucer he and his wife observed in the Berina mountains in 1952. Included in the series was this photo, which, when enlarged, revealed a "humanoid" near the UFO. Though attacked by the scientific establishment, Monguzzi courageously maintains his photos to be legitimate.

——September 17, near Cenon. A farmer met a very small being in a diving suit, who made friendly gestures and spoke in an "inhuman and incomprehensible" voice.

——October 11, near Taupignac. Three men observed a round machine with a dome hovering low, and saw four little men, about one meter (3 feet) tall, who were "busy" near their machine but quickly fled in their saucer at the intrusion.

Jacques Vallee gives these interesting data about his 200 cases of 1954:

—All of the sightings took place in rural areas, none in the regions of high density population.

—102 sightings, over half, were made by more than one witness. In 13 cases there were more than 10 witnesses, and in one case no less than 150 people.

—The average diameter of the landed UFO's was 5 meters (16.5 feet).

—Besides the low-flying saucers, 118 made actual landings.

—In 42 cases the UFOnauts were seen—5 inside and 37 outside their craft.

—In 10 cases the saucermen were of human or taller height.

—In 39 cases the saucermen were "dwarfs" usually a meter tall (about 3 feet).

—Altogether, 80 tiny men were seen. In one sighting, 7 dwarfs were seen entering one UFO and flying away.

The ratio of 39 sightings of "little men" out of 200 (20%) is impressive. And if an average of 2 tiny UFOnauts emerged from each landed UFO—including the low-flying craft, which presumably landed before or after —then some 400 "dwarfs" stepped out on the ground in the year 1954 (mainly in France, according to Jacques Vallee's specialized listing, which only briefly included a few other worldwide sightings).

South American UFOnauts

Gordon Creighton, also in *The Humanoids,* made the same analysis for South America from 1947 to 1965 and lists 65 cases in which "entities," or operators, were seen

emerging from landed saucers. His totals come out as follows:

—Giant Men 6
—Tall men (around 6 feet) 9
—Medium-sized or average men 5
—Tiny men from 2½ to 3½ feet tall 12
—Hairy and "bellicose" dwarfs 5
—Green-skinned little men 3
—Hairy Giant 1

Grouping all the undersized creatures together, we get
a total of 20 out of the 65 cases, by far the majority.
While most of the "little men" are described as "humanlike," some of them are quite different, and a few are
frightening:

——November 28, 1954, near Caracas, Venezuela.
Two truck drivers claimed to be "attacked" by a small
creature with raking claws and big, glowing eyes. When
one man drew a knife, the blade only glanced off the
dwarf's skin, which seemed as hard as steel.

——October 4, 1954, Salta, Argentina. Three
school children came upon "several creatures of short
stature, greenish skin, and remotely resembling human
beings."

Among the giant beings, too, are specimens of terrifying
appearance, such as:

—A tall creature with a melon-shaped head, very
long white hair, and "three eyes which stared fixedly
without blinking."

—A slim man over 6 feet tall who appeared to have
no ears or nose, had a vivid red complexion, and only
one large brown eye devoid of any eyebrow.

—A "luminous man totally surrounded by lights" so
dazzling they blinded the witness temporarily.

—Five "Martians" taller than men with only one
eye in the center of their foreheads.

—An entity of "greenish" color and with "hair all
covered with green lights and looking like a toad."

The mention of a half dozen monstrosities with single
eyes like the Cyclops, repeated nowhere else in the world,
makes one suspect that Latin imagination supplied a few

colorful details not really there.

Nondwarf UFOnauts

One category listed neither by Jacques Vallee nor Gordon Creighton is that of the "robots" or "robotlike" creatures sometimes reported:

——May 24, 1962, Province of La Pampa, Argentina. A woman was taken to a hospital in shock after saying she saw a landed saucer and two "robotlike" creatures near it.

——October 12, 1963, Province of Cordoba, Argentina. Eugenio Douglas, driving a truck, found the road blocked by a huge, metallic oval at least 30 feet high. Out of a side door emerged three huge "robots" in human form, about 25 feet tall and wearing helmets and short antennas "like the horns of a snail."

In the case of "humanlike" UFOnauts, they are often described as being "tall, blond, and with long hair." This is repeated often enough, in both Vallee's and Creighton's sightings as well as other listings, to look suspiciously like another "pattern."

Other patterns that seem to emerge from the UFOnaut sightings raise some puzzling questions:

A) Does the variety of saucermen, from dwarfs to human-sized creatures to monstrous giants, indicate that the spacecraft of more than one world are visiting earth?

B) Why are the "hairy dwarfs" always bellicose, while the other little men are peaceful?

C) Why do some wear "diving suits" or other paraphernalia like an astronaut's spacesuit, while others are clad in simple "parkas" or "coveralls" and seem to breathe our air without harm?

Reliability of Reports

However, one outstanding pattern does emerge that helps to make viable the case for the UFO's—the increasing numbers of ground sightings of the nonhairy "little men" who are all of similar height and of human propor-

ons, and who often seem to be gathering specimens of
arth's soil, plants, and animal life.

Most of the reports in both Vallee's and Creighton's
sts come from "hinterland" people—farmers, woods-
en, laborers, small-town or rural officials and such.
Many of them never heard the word "flying saucer" or
UFO" before, being out of touch with the world at
arge.

It is unreasonable to suppose that all of them had read
or heard of previous little-men reports in the other coun-
ries and had therefore merely "copied" this description
or illusory phenomena involving saucers that landed.

Jacques Vallee, in *The Humanoids*, makes this statement about the French UFO observers he had personally
interviewed: "In the 1954 landings, the spectrum of witnesses is typically rural, with a normal proportion of men,
women, and children. Most witnesses held steady jobs,
often positions of social responsibility, and observed an
unusual phenomenon while engaged in their usual occu-
pations and in their usual environment."

He emphasizes this in order to refute any claims by
anti-UFO skeptics that his witnesses were the "crackpot"
or irresponsible element of France. When dozens of
sober, solid citizens of any country or region experience
sightings, no matter how "wild," their reports, too, must
be sober and solid. It is absurd to claim that perfectly
normal people consistently make abnormal reports.

It has been one of the major faults of the U.S. Air
Force, bordering on stupidity, to constantly ridicule witnesses in America, hinting they saw "illusions" or had
one drink too many. Only the witnesses, not the Air
Force people, saw what was reported. Therefore, how can
the Air Force "analysts" give any sort of opinion or make
any judgment of phenomena unseen by them? It is the
old story of the giraffe—"there is no such animal."

Pygmy Pattern

It may very well be, as proposed in *The Humanoids*,
that the little-men sightings have actually gone on all the

time, and all around the world, probably for centurie
past. One has only to think of the almost universal leg
ends among mankind of the gnomes, trolls, kobolds, fair
ies, leprechauns, pixies, peri, *et al.,* to suspect that thes
tales arose when flying saucers landed and the dwarfis
saucermen came out—and almost always at *night,* if w
go by today's reports.

If so, the patterned evidence becomes strong indee
that the UFO's are genuine flying machines whose pilo
are often pygmy men.

CHAPTER 11

Intelligent Control

July 16, 1964, Houghton Lake, Michigan. Kenneth Jannereth, a pilot for Northern Air Service, reported to the Air Force that he had observed six UFO's when he was 15 miles south of Houghton Lake.

First, four objects appeared at about 11:00 P.M., coming up rapidly, and Jannereth, alarmed, was about to take evasive action to avoid collision. But the UFO's swung around to his left, pacing him.

Then two more bright lights appeared and the six unknowns stayed off his wing and followed him for five minutes. They were only 200 to 300 feet away—circular and not fuzzy. Two UFO's were above his wing, two on line with his plane, and two below his wing, an echelon formation that they kept up with precision.

The pilot was most impressed by the rapid approach of the UFO's and their sudden deceleration. He had never seen anything like it and felt that the objects "were definitely being flown by someone with intelligence." (From *"The Reference."*)

INTELLIGENT CONTROL—THESE are the key words to the above sighting and to innumerable others. If critics insist that all landing reports and "little men" are to be discounted as too fantastic, then what about the impressive evidence that the UFO's, during flight without landing, are under the control of rational beings, whether little men or not?

Time and again, this *pattern of intelligent control* has been implicit, if not explicit, in saucer reports. The following cases demonstrate this point to a remarkable degree:

——August 12, 1953, near Rapid City, South Dakota. An F-84 was scrambled to follow a UFO and chased it for 120 miles. Both the UFO and the jet were plainly seen on a radar screen below. Each time the jet began to close in, the UFO would move ahead with a burst of speed. When the pilot gave up and turned back to base, the UFO promptly turned around, also, and followed, until a second jet arrived, causing the object to leave at high speed.

——November 1953, Ski, Norway. Tryggve Jansen, a paint contractor, and his wife were motoring when they saw a luminous object maneuvering above a bridge. Then it zoomed down at the car, making several close passes. He says, " 'Another thing like that and I stop the car,' I told my wife. Just as if my words had been comprehended by the driver of the strange craft, it made an abrupt turn and kept right toward us. It came down over the road, some ten meters (33 feet) in front of us. It did not land on the road but hovered a bit above it. . . . When 'landing,' the craft had executed an elegant right-about-turn. All of its movements seemed to be consciously calculated and intelligently executed. . . . I had an intense feeling that something or somebody within gazed at (us). . . ."

——April 3, 1964, Monticello, Wisconsin. A graduate student in anthropology was driving with his wife and two in-laws when they spied a weird object like a platform and tower, hung with lights—a sort of "flying hatrack." The UFO hovered and maneuvered above the car for a while, and the witnesses stated that it "appeared interested in the car" and gave indication of being under intelligent operation.

Curiosity Seekers

What is actually demonstrated in the above cases is *inquisitiveness,* an attribute we can assume is common to all intelligent minds on earth or elsewhere. Obviously, in the first case, the UFO pilot was testing the performance of the jet or perhaps testing the abilities of the jet pilot. In the other cases, the saucers may have been taking pictures of the cars below or otherwise tabulating data with sensors.

Other striking signs of curiosity, or inquisitive examination of things earthly, occur in the following cases:

—A glowing elliptical UFO approached an airliner and circled it, completely stopping once on each side, then speeding away.

—Two discs approached from the horizon while tipped on edge, and circled a big Skyhook research balloon for some time before leaving.

—A disc followed a British jet to its airfield and hovered overhead to see the jet land, after which it sped away.

—A luminous disc followed a car with a distance of only 100 yards between them, and slowed down or speeded up whenever the car did.

—A disc with four body lights circled the town of Millville, New Jersey, in a leisurely fashion until the beam of a searchlight hit it, whereupon the UFO fled.

—A blinding bright UFO came down, killing a truck's engine via some EM effect, then hovered overhead for 3 or 4 minutes before departing.

—A luminous disc shot toward a plane at great speed, then circled it and followed it for an hour.

Reacting UFOnauts

Another attribute that only intelligence can display—not the blind forces of nature or any programmed robot device—is *reaction* to environment and its stimuli. Note the quick and definite response of the UFO in each of the cases ahead:

——A ball of light approached an airliner and hovered nearby. When the pilot switched on all cabin lights for a better look, the UFO instantly took off.

——A round UFO floated over a Florida missile range at 3,000 feet. When a Marine jet banked toward it, the saucer accelerated out of sight in seconds.

——A cylindrical UFO swung lazily over a South African air base. When their searchlights stabbed toward it, the saucer "withdrew" behind clouds.

Human beings make a move, and the UFO reacts with

trigger-touch rapidity. Only watching pairs of alien eyes could so patently avoid close inspection. Illusions or mirages do not take "evasive action." Only machines guided by intelligent hands will account for this kind of awareness and behavior.

Controlled Power

Powered flight under control is another criterion by which we can infer that an intelligent entity guides the UFO's. When an object exhibits intricate maneuvers in the sky, never possible to fixed stars, meteors, balloons, birds, or earthly aircraft, it can be only a machine fed by some kind of power plant aboard the craft.

Note the following comments by professional people:

—"It was man-made, as evidenced by the outline and functional appearance." Technicians at Edwards AFB, California, who observed a UFO that "cavorted" overhead and performed "incredible maneuvers."

—"The remarkably sudden ascent convinced me it was an absolutely novel airborne *device*" (his italics). An astronomer in New Mexico who witnessed a smooth elliptical UFO that accelerated up into clouds at 600 to 900 mph.

—"The clouds were drifting from the southwest to the northeast, at right angles to the motion of the object. Therefore, it must have been powered in some way." Dr. Seymour L. Hess, head of the Department of Meteorology of Florida State University, when he saw a UFO from the grounds of Lowell Observatory in Arizona.

The fantastic maneuvers of other saucers in the air have been utterly breathtaking, according to the observers, which indicates a machine of immense power guided by thinking creatures:

—A bright orange light that hovered, bobbed around and arced back and forth, up and down.

—A glowing cigar that dove down, leveled off, made a sharp left turn, climbed steeply, and shot away.

—A yellow-orange light that rapidly "pulsated,"

made square turns, sudden stops and starts, and used bursts of great speed in between.

—A silvery egg-shaped UFO that hovered, made violent "jerks" up and down, rocked back and forth, and finally darted away.

Such reports of UFO's accelerating at blinding speeds, making impossible right-angle turns, reversing direction in one instant, diving down from space to stop abruptly and hover, weaving through the sky in intricate looping patterns—all these are close to clear-cut evidence of powered vehicles whose masters fully control all movements with consummate skill.

And when it is *purposeful* movement, such as following a jet or circling a city, it precludes any conceivable kind of natural object and almost conclusively proves that it is an artificial flying machine made by beings with engineering minds.

If not, how would the UFO skeptics explain these astounding phenomena?

Saucer Formations

Another manifestation of UFO's being steered by unknown intelligences is when they fly in group formation and perform precise maneuvers in unison. The word "precise" eliminates flocks of birds, floating pieces of paper, lost kites, clusters of weather balloons, or any other objects known to man.

"Fleets" of two or more UFO's are well documented in hundreds of sightings, of which some typical samples are these:

———July 14, 1952, Newport News, Viriginia. A flight of six in-line UFO's, plus two "pacers," flipped over in a 120-degree turn without breaking formation.

———August 1, 1952, Albuquerque, New Mexico. Ten UFO's shifted formation with perfect precision, from a cluster to a V-formation, then two abreast.

———August 1956, Boulder City, Nevada. Five discs flew over in a staggered-V formation, exactly one diameter apart, and never varied a hairline.

All of these sightings, if taken seriously by any anti-UFO scoffer, would be difficult to explain in any conceivable way other than that a guiding hand and mind within the strange saucers enables them to perform such sky tricks.

Mind-made Machines

Besides intelligent control and evidences of powered flight, one other factor tends to place the stamp of manufactured machinery on UFO's—the structural details often reported during close or prolonged sightings. These would include metallic hulls, windows or portholes, antennas or "booms," lamps and searchlights, or any rotating part of the UFO. All of them are almost sure signs of a vehicle designed and built by living entities, not something that "just grew" or formed out of amorphous matter in some way.

An overwhelming proportion of sightings specify one or more of such structural features, as in the cases herewith:

——November 7, 1951, over Lake Superior. A bright orange oval was observed with 6 portholes spaced in two rows on the UFO's underside.

——September 16, 1952, Belle Glade, Florida. A circular disc had distinct red and white lights spaced alternately around the outside rim on the underside.

——February 2, 1955, Venezuela. A saturnlike disc was seen rotating, from an airliner. The UFO also had rows of windows on the upper and lower domes.

——November 5, 1955, Cleveland, Ohio. Seen by hundreds as it slowly cruised over the city, an elliptical UFO clearly displayed 8 windows.

——February 19, 1952, Kilimanjaro, Africa. A cigar-shaped UFO was seen hovering for 15 minutes, with bands of metal circling it.

——Summer 1952, Martin County, Texas. An object like "two turtle shells stuck together and joined by a rim" was also seen to have a slit from which two "paddles" (booms) extended that slowly waved back and forth.

———August 25, 1957, Pittsburg, Kansas. A platter-shaped object had windows at the top, and around the rim was a series of small "propellers" about 6 inches long, rotating at high speed.

———July 22, 1963, Parr, England. Two boys saw a bell-shaped UFO with a "periscope" sticking out, also two "rods" and a "tripod landing gear" at the bottom.

———April 3, 1964, Monticello, Wisconsin. A UFO seen by four people was like a rectangular platform with lights at the corners, plus a tall "tower" also lit up (as mentioned previously).

Most of these sightings were made at close range, often within 100 yards and sometimes within 100 feet. Some are daytime sightings, but even at night an object with bright lights or a luminous glow would reveal the reported details in a close sighting.

One of the most famed observations was made by Dr. Clyde Tombaugh, discoverer of the planet Pluto, who saw glowing rectangular "windows" moving across the sky in such a way that he believed they were part of a dimmer bulk behind them—namely, a UFO with portholes.

Silent Saucers

A sort of "negative" proof of the reality of UFO's is their uncanny *silence* in most sightings of medium or distant range (the low whines and hums and other noises usually come from close-range objects).

The lack of sound proves that they are not earth-made craft, for all our prop-planes, jets, helicopters, blimps, and rockets make an infernal racket when cutting through the air. As for falling meteorites or natural fireballs, they are always accompanied by ear-shattering blasts or high-decibel roarings.

Nothing known to man can move through dense air in high-velocity maneuvers with ghostlike silence—except strange, unidentified vehicles with some noise-free type of propulsion and a method of eliminating the screech of air friction. In almost every sighting (95% or more) any-

where on earth in the past 20 years, the remarks of the
witnesses are similar:

—"I heard no slightest sound."

—"It moved around in eerie silence."

—"No noise at all accompanied its amazing flight."

—"I turned off my car motor and listened intently,
but all was utterly quiet."

—"It wasn't any sound that made me look up, but
the intense bright glow overhead that I saw out of the
corner of my eye."

—"The UFO swooped maybe a thousand feet above
me, but I couldn't hear the slightest engine noise, not
even the 'whoosh' of its fast movement through the
air."

Then there's the lack of "sonic booms" associated with
the flight of supersonic UFO's. The "skyquakes" reported-
ly heard around the times of UFO sightings, which are
much louder than the sonic booms of jetcraft, are thought
to be either some phenomenon associated with a saucer's
"projection of power" for some purpose or may unfortunately be a UFO exploding when its cushioning electromagnetic field collapses and the machine suddenly meets
the full brunt of air resistance. (See previous chapter on
propulsion.)

But like silent phantoms, most UFO's glide and slice
through our atmosphere without creating sound waves,
which certainly proves—if they are truly machines—that
they were designed and manufactured by intellects not of
this earth.

Extraterrestrial Vehicles

"Reliable reports indicate there are objects
coming into our atmosphere at very high speeds
and controlled by thinking intelligences. . . ."
—Admiral Delmer Fahrney, former USN Missile
Chief.

"One thing is absolutely certain. We're being
watched by beings from outer space. . . ."—
Albert M. Chop, former Air Force press official
for handling UFO news.

"I believe extraterrestrial intelligences are

watching the earth and have been visiting us for
millennia in their flying saucers. . . ."—
Professor Hermann Oberth.

"Flying saucers come from another
world. . . ."—Dr. Hideo Itokawa, Japanese
scientist.

"I believe the flying saucers come from outer
space, piloted by beings of superior
intelligence. . . ."—William Lear, President of
Lear Inc.

These unequivocal statements from eminent authorities
probably represent the feelings of many more VIP's who
do not dare to speak out. The "outer space pattern" has
the most adherents, both among UFOLogists and technical experts, who, after analyzing thousands of reports,
can come only to that logical conclusion.

However, Dr. Jacques Vallee warns us (*Challenge to
Science: The UFO Enigma*) that we should not "jump to
conclusions" about the saucerians being interstellar trav-
elers. Some of the UFO data are so macabre and inexplicable that we may, he suggests, be dealing with a phenomenon entirely unknown to our science. The universe
may be a much more complex place than we suspect,
with planes or levels of possible life and mental entities of
which we cannot even conceive.

He cautions that the true scientific attitude is to go
only by the firm facts and the bare data given in sightings, without too much extrapolation into realms of pure
guesswork. We do not yet have, he points out, enough
solid information to make any valid assumptions on the
origin of the UFO's and their presumed operators.

Wise counsel. This book, to repeat, though it gives
some of the theoretical extrapolations, has the sole purpose of trying to show that UFO's *exist*—nothing more
—by virtue of the significant "patterns" that have been
reviewed.

Anti-Saucer Syndrome

In this chapter we have several subpatterns—intelligent
control, inquisitiveness, reaction, group flight, intricate

sky maneuvers, powered machines, presence of portholes and other structural details, silent flight—which all form a single master pattern of *mind-made saucers* as the answer to the riddle of the UFO's.

This is perhaps the greatest stumbling block to acceptance of UFO's by scientists and other authorities. Arrogant mankind seems to hate to admit that there can be *superior* minds beyond earth.

In his book *The Flying Saucer Conspiracy* (Holt, New York, 1955) Donald Keyhoe quotes from the *American Scandinavian Magazine,* November 15, 1953, giving the words of F. Schilp Haman:

"When anything fundamentally new comes up there are hoaxes, rumors, controversies, name-calling, and even persecutions. . . .

"There have been many blows to the ego of men on this sad little planet, but through it all there persisted the fond belief that mentally we were still out in front, still on top.

"One thing is certain. The human race won't lightly give up the feeling of security it cherishes, or the pet superstition that it constitutes the acme of intelligence in the universe. This monopoly of brains it believes it has is a deep-seated, near-religious conviction."

And, of necessity, the wish-it-away syndrome must strike scientists in particular, for they are purportedly the "best" minds on earth. Hence, they will, in general—with notable exceptions—stubbornly resist the reality of UFO's, because along with that admission would come the devastating realization that they are no longer the "best" minds in the universe.

Scientists would then face the prospect of having to compete with, or be compared to, far greater mentalities from extraterrestrial or nonearthly sources. It is human nature to hold on to positions of eminence. And, after all, scientists are human, if not open-minded.

It seems quite obvious that the only people whose minds are not closed to the possibility of manned saucers from elsewhere are mainly nonscientific people from all other walks of life.

And every scientist—their numbers grow daily—who already concedes the reality of UFO phenomena is therefore to be greatly commended, for he has had to fight earth-oriented prejudice and has also risked his reputation with his austere and disapproving colleagues.

"As for the professional scientists," wrote Dr. Jacques Vallee (*Challenge* to *Science: the UFO Enigma*), "to brush away such accounts (the Premanon, France, landing of a UFOnaut) with a smile is for them one of the tests of fashion. This silence in high places should disturb us greatly."

Aimé Michel puts it more bluntly (*Flying Saucers and the Straight-Line Mystery*): "What is astonishing, and I may even say scandalous, is that scientists should have been content to base their conclusions . . . on newspaper reports of (an) irresponsible kind."

But no matter. If the *pattern of intelligence* behind the saucers proves true, then sooner or later all scientific doubting Thomases on earth will have to take their medicine, the bitterer because it was not taken sooner.

If this "indictment" of science, in general, seems unwarranted, it is even more unwarranted for scientists to continue their blind and often violent opposition to the UFO phenomenon. Science, in the first place, means investigation of *new phenomena* regardless of whether they fit into current theory or not. Theories are made to be discarded when outworn.

In this respect, the UFO phenomenon has shone down a harsh light, revealing that most "scientists" today do not deserve the name. They have deserted true science in the case of the flying saucer riddle.

CHAPTER 12

Missions of Mystery

—November 14, 1954, in Isola (near La Soezia, Northern Italy). A farmer saw a bright cigar-shaped craft land near him and hid himself.

From the machine came three dwarfs dressed in metallic diving suits, who centered their attention on rabbits in their cages while speaking among themselves in a strange tongue.

Thinking they planned to steal the animals, the farmer slipped away, returned with a rifle, and aimed at the dwarfs.

Then two things happened: first, the rifle failed, and at the same time it became so heavy that the farmer had to drop it.

He also found that he was unable to move or speak, while the intruders took the rabbits and left, their craft leaving a bright trail. As they departed, the farmer was able to move again. . . .

(From "The Pattern Behind the UFO Landings" by Dr. Jacques Vallee, in *The Humanoids*.)

ONLY A FEW scattered accounts like this one mentioned precisely what the UFOnauts who land on earth were doing. The rest is an unknown, leaving unanswered the big question—just *why* are the saucerians here on earth?

UFO Types

The various types of saucer-craft form a pattern, admittedly speculative, that might be a clue to their purpose in visiting our planet. The breakdown might be as follows:

A) Giant cigar-shaped *"mother ships"* hang at high altitudes and are often seen releasing smaller craft that go below. These huge UFO's are presumably the true interstellar ships that cross the gulfs of space from another star.

All the others are short-range craft with specialized functions in and around earth.

B) Most often released from the mother ships, the *discs* then "scout" below, later returning to their parent craft, which would account for the many "straight-up" flights seen by witnesses.

C) More often seen at night, the glowing *spheroids* and *ovoids* perhaps are on photographic missions of city lights and installations.

D) The odd-shaped craft carrying many lights and often shining down searchlight beams could logically be *observation UFO's*.

E) All other saucer types—triangular, rocketlike, etc. —would be on special missions of an unguessable nature.

F) The *landers* are usually *disclike*, under 50 feet in diameter, from which step forth the "little men" who seemingly make close observations of our life and pick up samples of earthly things.

This arbitrary classification might be (and probably is) totally wrong except perhaps for the class "A" objects. There is hardly any other explanation that could cover the fact that they have often been seen to eject and then gather in small UFO's. One organization (NICAP) prefers to call them "satellite objects," meaning they are large craft with smaller attendant craft.

Mother Ships

Besides the spectacular and well-witnessed pair of "cigar" sightings in France in 1952 (Chapter 2), the following account also shows the great wonder and excitement any sighting of a mother ship arouses in the witness:

——September 8, 1958, Offutt AFB, Omaha, Nebraska, as reported by Major Paul A. Duich, USAF (ret.) to NICAP: ". . . I could see it through the window as I talked to a tower operator. The glow was now diminishing. . . . The fuzzy appearance gradually took on a solid look, in the distinct shape of a pencil or slender cigar. The upper end was blunter than the lower end . . . All of a sudden we all (10 or 20 other officers) started checking each others' faces for some silly reason—for assurance of reality, perhaps. For as we watched there appeared at the lower end of the object a swarm of black specks cavorting every which way, much like a swarm of gnats. . . ."

——August 23, 1954, Vernon, France. Bernard Miserey, a businessman, was surprised to see a huge, silent, luminous mass in the night sky that looked like a gigantic cigar standing on end . . . "I had been watching this amazing spectacle for a couple of minutes when suddenly, from the bottom of the 'cigar' came an object like a horizontal disc. . . . It was surrounded by a halo of brilliant light. A few minutes (later) a similar object came from the 'cigar' and went

A cigar-shaped "mother ship," like those that dozens of reliable witnesses have reported seeing.

through the same maneuvers. A third object came, then a fourth . . . and finally a fifth disc detached itself from the cigar. . . . It wobbled like the first four and took off like a flash toward the north, where it was lost in the distance. . . . During this time the luminosity of the 'cigar' had faded, and the gigantic object, which may have been three hundred feet long, had sunk into darkness. . . . The spectacle had lasted about three quarters of an hour." (From *"The Reference."*)

ther Satellite Objects

But not all of these satellite-objects are of the cigar or lindrical shape, as the following brief cases show:

———October, 1951, Anderson, Indiana. The parent object (mother ship) was a wing-shaped UFO trailed by over 30 small, dark objects.

———1952, San Mateo, California. Satellite object was a flat oval that emitted 5 smaller objects.

———January 11, 1958, Vista, California. Parent object, spindle-shaped, released 8 to 10 smaller craft of the same shape.

———May 3, 1961, Toonpang, NSW, Australia. A round, domed mother ship ejected 4 small silvery V-shaped objects that maneuvered at high speed, then returned to the parent craft.

In certain cases the cigar-type mother ship seems like a uge "cloud," or partly obscured by a cloudy haze lit by n eerie glow that sometimes fades away, cigar and all. his may be a different kind of UFO phenomenon, to be ken up in another chapter.

But there seems little doubt that the satellite objects e giant space "carriers" that have probably hauled their roods of smaller craft through interstellar space. Many f the cigars have been seen moving at prodigious veloc-y high in rarefied atmosphere—commonly over 5,000 ph and sometimes at orbital speed of 18,000 mph, indiating they hang above earth 50 miles high or more at mes.

As to size, some are unbelievable, as per this accou (data from *The True Report on Flying Saucers,* compil by the editors of *True,* Fawcett Publications, 1967):

From August 19, 1949, to March 10, 1950, on 10 differe occasions, a powerful 8-million-candle-power searchlig caught a glowing round object four or five miles high. Tw groups of five smaller objects, shaped like Indian arrowhea were seen emerging from this "space station," whose diam ter was calculated to be no less than 10,000 feet——*t miles wide.*

Maybe even the big disc-emitting cigars (100 to 1,0(feet long) are not the true stellar ships and, in turn, ne tle within such cyclopean "space stations" that have t power to ram across the immensity of space at incompr hensible speeds.

UFO "Scouts"

Among the small craft emitted by the big mother shi; are the UFO's that apparently make no landings but pe form odd and breathtaking sky maneuvers or strea across the skies at incredible speeds. It is sheer gues work, but perhaps they are on missions to map the eart photograph big cities, analyze the lower air, or condu other scientific tests.

But three classes of craft carry on missions whose pu pose we can surmise. One of them we might call the "ol server UFO's," for they quite obviously hover over citie installations, power stations, and other earthly sites as examining them thoroughly with scientific sensors.

And this gives us another pattern of UFO activity th; takes it out of the realm of random or chance ph nomena. A remarkable number of sightings are over bodi of water—lakes, reservoirs, rivers, and such. Notab among them are the sightings at Wanaque Dam in Ne Jersey, where throughout most of 1965 and 1966 variou UFO's were spotted by the local police patrols. Always th UFO's hovered or darted over the water, sometimes send ing down dazzling searchlight beams.

Just why are the UFO's so interested in our water su; plies? Again we draw a blank, for we cannot even guess.

Saucer over San Francisco: taken by Joe Kerska on October 10, 1956. *Considered authentic.*

Another significant group of saucers hangs around power lines and electrical stations, which led to the famed Exeter, New Hampshire, sightings in 1965-66, as thoroughly researched by John Fuller in his book *Incident at Exeter.*

Just why are the UFO's so interested in our power stations? And did they *cause* various electrical "blackouts," as some UFOlogists have suggested? This theory even includes the great Northeastern blackout of November 9, 1965, when 30 million people in eight states and two Canadian provinces were deprived of power for many hours. Some 23 sightings of saucers were reported on that day from Canada down to New Jersey, hovering over power lines and power stations. Whether they somehow engineered the blackout or merely observed this interesting event after it happened by itself, nobody knows.

But the most significant pattern of observing UFO's is

the large number of hovering saucers and green fireballs sighted in the southwestern states over our atomic installations and missile ranges. More on that in the next chapter.

Observation Saucers

The second class of UFO's whose activity seems plain are the saucers that chase cars, trucks, trains, planes, ships at sea, and even individual persons or families. Their purpose is seemingly to test out speed and performance of our various vehicles and to study human behavior, as in the following cases:

——July 28, 1954, at sea off New York, New York. A UFO, with spots of light around it, hovered and followed a Dutch ship about 40° off the port bow, then shot up into the clouds.

——June 6, 1956, Banning, California. Driving, a salesman saw a bubble-topped disc hovering over his car, and when he stopped, the saucer deliberately circled him in a weaving motion before suddenly darting away.

——October 3, 1958, North Central Indiana. A train crew for an hour and 10 minutes saw 4 saucer discs following their long freight train, sometimes speeding ahead, sometimes behind, and often alongside the cars, as if inspecting them.

Some experiences where people are being "shadowed" by a UFO can be unnerving, as in the following incident:

December 21, 1957, Fonta Poran, Brazil. Mrs. Ivonne Torres de Mendonca, her three children, a servant, and the driver of their jeep were making their way along a deserted road at night, when two large, round UFO's came swooping down and followed them, each on one side of the road.

Terrified, they stopped the jeep, whereupon the UFO's also stopped and hovered. When the group again drove on, the objects immediately followed them, one of them shining a brilliant light down on the people at times, while the other flew close overhead, as if observing them minutely.

The nightmarish chase lasted for 2 long hours until the jeep reached a town where, after observing the vehicle's tank

eing filled with gas, the two UFO's sped away at tremendous
peed. (From *"The Reference."*)

Most numerous of all are the instances where planes
re followed by UFO's, the saucers sometimes pacing
hem steadily, other times playing "tag" with jet pilots.
The following cases, are representative of this class of "ae-
ial reconnaissance UFO's":

———January 29, 1952, Wonsan, Korea. A saucer
paralleled a USAF bomber for 5 minutes, then pulled
ahead and shot away at an angle.

———August 12, 1953, Rapid City, South Dakota. A
luminous UFO was chased by an F-84. When the jet
turned back, the UFO turned and followed until a second jet gave chase.

———August 28, 1952, Leroy, New York. A saucer
disc made a series of "tight circles" around an airliner.

———June 30, 1954, near Goose Bay, Labrador (this is
one of the "classic" cases). A large dark UFO with
smaller objects around it paced a BOAC airliner for
85 miles.

———July 14, 1959, Minas Gerais State, Brazil. A
luminous UFO followed a Brazilian Air Force B-26 all
the way to its base and hovered over the airport to
watch the plane land, before zooming away.

People Watchers

Among the most weird and spine-chilling cases are
those in which a UFO observes people on the ground,
like germs under a microscope:

———September 20, 1962, Hawthorne, New Jersey.
An object with two body lights hovered over a quarry
at night. When the watchman got nervous at being
"observed" and flashed on his jeep's headlights, the
UFO fled.

———May 11, 1950, McMinnville, Oregon. Mr. and
Mrs. Paul Trent found a domed disc hovering and slowly drifting over their farmhouse and barn. If the UFO
was photographing them, Mrs. Trent was doing the
same in return and obtained five excellent photos.

———August 5, 1963, Fairfield, Illinois. A farm fam-

ily in Wayne County cowered in their darkened home
while a brilliant light cruised over their farm for several hours. The UFO cast down a dazzling glare and
seemed to be examining their property minutely and
perhaps waiting for the humans to emerge to be looked
over carefully (courtesy of *Saucers, Space & Science*
#33, produced by Gene Duplantier, Willowdale, On-
tario, Canada).

——October 14, 1954, Meral, France. A farmer in
his fields at dusk saw an orange-colored ball land on the
ground not far away, after which a blinding light was

George Stock took a series of photos of a UFO near his
home in Passaic, New Jersey. Stock used a Brownie camera,
had the prints developed through the local drugstore.

turned on that illuminated the farmer and his fields for 200 yards around for some 10 minutes.

The classic case, however, is the celebrated "kidnapping" of Barney and Betty Hill in September 1961, as described in detail in the book *Interrupted Journey,* by John Fuller. Returning from a trip, the Hills saw a UFO following their car in New Hampshire and stopped. A group of "undersized" beings with odd, slanting eyes and mouth-slits seemingly "hypnotized" them, took them aboard their saucer for physical examinations, then released them without any memory of their experience, though they noticed they arrived home two hours late.

Later, under regressive hypnosis by a psychiatrist, the Hills slowly began to recall the above experiences in detail, including descriptions of the interior of the ship, the examining instruments, and the "telepathic" speech used by the saucerians.

This is the one "contactee" story that is the exception to the rule and may be authentic. Certainly the Hills wanted to avoid all publicity and had to be coaxed into revealing their amazing experience before the book could be written—a characteristic quite opposite of all other contactees, who avidly search out the limelight, eager to tell their very dubious tales of meeting the UFOnauts in person. Hence, we can place some credence in the word of the Hills, though it might still be an obscure psychological phenomenon in which they had a mutual "dream" or "hallucination."

Humanoid Missions

Now we come to the third group of UFO's whose "missions" seem fairly obvious, involving saucers that land to let the UFOnaut little men out. The details are usually skimpy but clear-cut, as in the cases that follow:

——July 22, 1963, Lancashire, England. Three youths saw a saucer, with a rotating and flashing light on top, that landed in the fields. Then a hatch slid open at the bottom, and what looked like a "periscope" came out, which swiveled around and "pointed at us" for a short time, after which the UFO left.

——October 28, 1962, near Adelaide, Australia Mrs. E. D. Sylvester, a teacher, was driving with he three children when they saw an egg-shaped vehicle, 1 feet long, land in a field. Stopping, they came upon tiny man in a "diving suit," holding some kind o "box" and taking soil samples at various spots for 4 minutes.

——December 19, 1954, Valencia, Venezuela. Jos Parra at dawn saw 6 little men hauling boulders from alongside a road into their disc saucer, which wa "parked" 9 feet above the ground.

——1954, Italy, as reported in *Life*. An Italia woman saw two "merry" little men, about 3 feet tall who descended from a "spool-shaped" object and stol from her some flowers and a pair of stockings, which were presumably hanging on the wash line.

——April 1, 1963, Marin County, California. A rancher, Louis Montanos, reported to the sheriff that huge disc had landed on his ranch and several smal men scurried out and seized a calf, bringing it int their craft. Emerging again with containers, they col lected samples of turf and other plants, then beckoned the rancher himself to come aboard. When he ran i fright they pursued a short way, then gave up and re turned to their saucer, shooting upward at great speed. Other missions, in brief, are revealed by a few word or sentences in certain sightings:

—"The ground seemed to have been dug up."

—"Small trees near the river were found cut up, ap parently with a knife."

—"The little man got out, scooped up a bucket o water in a shiny pail, and handed it to someone insid the saucer-craft."

—"One of the tiny men held a dark-colored chai or stick which gave off blue-white sparks."

—"Two little men and two little women tried t grab his dog, who growled and bit one of them, so the left."

—Two small men gathered trays of soil from a field

and also took a bag of fertilizer from a farm.

Saucerian Communications

It would seem, from the above, that a systematic study is being made of the earth's fauna and flora by the little saucermen who land here and there around the world. In very few cases did they threaten any human being or attempt to "kidnap" him as in the Montanos case. In most other incidents the UFOnauts fled as soon as they found themselves observed by their human hosts.

Oddly enough, though it seems that the general policy of the saucermen is to *avoid* contact or communication with us, there are a few cases where they seemed more "friendly":

——September 1, 1965, Huánuco, Peru. A workman in a field came upon an oval-shaped UFO parked on the ground, from which emerged a "dwarf" with a head twice as large as normal, who waved his arms as if trying to communicate by "sign language" with the workman. When the workman failed to understand, the creature gave up and flew off in his saucer.

——September 20, 1965, Puno, Brazil. A shepherd girl reported six little men stepping out of a landed UFO who made honking sounds and "talked as if they were geese." Failing to understand them, she fled in fright.

——March 9, 1967, Shamokin, Pennsylvania. Forrest Kerstetter and his wife, while driving up a mountain, spied an object flying low with an "enormous row of lights . . . flashing like a theater marquee. . . . I got out of the car with a spotlight and flashed some signals to it—three shorts and a long. Immediately the row of lights went out, and the huge lower lights flashed back the same signal to me—five or six times. Then all the other lights turned on. . . . It went off."

——November 11, 1955, San Bernardino, California. When a pilot blinked his landing lights twice, the UFO responded by blinking twice. The pilot then blinked three times and so did the saucer, after which it "backed up" in the air and shot away.

Semicontactee Claims

These isolated and brief encounters, with possible signals and attempted messages between people and the UFOnauts, hardly represent a concerted effort by the saucerians to establish communications with earth but are merely "byplay" incidents. The flying saucer operators have given the consistent impression for 20 years of wanting to avoid direct contact with us.

For that reason, we must view with suspicion the sightings in which the UFOnauts purportedly tried to establish direct communication or even spoke in some earth language. Though these are not actually "contactee" cases in their full sense, they are borderline as to authenticity:

———In Scotland a UFOnaut "conversed" with a man he met, using sign language, who said he was from Mars.

———In Mexico two little men 4½ feet tall spoke "good Spanish but in a strange accent" to a man they met and led him to their ship, inviting him aboard. He declined and they left.

———In Argentina a voice from a disc-UFO reputedly told a man that it was an interplanetary spacecraft and the space people had a base nearby and would soon show themselves to the whole world.

———A Brazilian claims a tiny UFOnaut 2½ feet tall gave him a piece of strange metal from his world.

———Perhaps the most extravagant report of all comes from a young Brazilian farmer who told of being "kidnapped" by four small men and brought aboard their UFO, where he was then forced to have sexual relations with a female member of their crew.

But these tall tales must never prejudice us against the much more sensible and believable reports about the little men from flying saucers.

Multiple Patterns

In this chapter several kinds of *patterns* have emerged

that are important in the UFO controversy. These patterns are:

—Mother ships releasing "scoutcraft" that descend to "explore" earth, presumably.

—"Reconnaissance UFO's" that hover over man-made landmarks and installations, water reservoirs, and power plants.

—Low-level UFO's that pursue or observe our vehicles and people themselves.

—Landing UFO's and little UFOnauts who collect samples of earthly plants and even animals, as well as inanimate objects and artifacts.

All these subpatterns merge into one main pattern—that UFO flights follow a "master plan" of movements and operations under *intelligent control*. Even the meager bits of sightings data about UFO activities add up dramatically to some sort of systematic survey of earth and its civilization, as we shall see in a chapter ahead.

CHAPTER 13

Hostile or Harmless?

July 1, 1954, Griffis AFB, New York. At noon the radarmen picked up an unauthorized blip on their screens. An F-94 Starfire was scrambled to check on the unknown, now near Utica, New York. The plane's radar observer soon spotted their target, after which they saw it visually—a strange, gleaming UFO. They closed in to investigate more closely.

Suddenly an intense wave of heat filled the cockpit. The pilot, glancing at his instruments, could see no warning of their engine or tanks being on fire.

The heat became like the blast of a furnace. At any moment it seemed the plane would burst into flames.

"Bail out . . . bail out!" yelled the pilot.

The two-man crew used their ejection seats, and both men safely descended by parachute. But they groaned, looking below. Their plane was crashing into the heart of a town—Walesville. It later proved that four people were killed by the falling jet.

After interrogation the two airmen were exonerated, having acted according to Air Force rules. There was no question that only fierce, unbearable heat had driven them out of their plane.

And there was little doubt that only one thing could have caused that mysterious "invisible fire" within their cockpit—the UFO they had been chasing. (Based on report in Air Force files).

WAS THE ABOVE incident an actual act of *aggression* on the part of the saucer? UFOlogists in general are divided into two camps on whether the alien beings in the UFO's are here on a hostile or a friendly mission. Both sides marshal up "evidence" to support their claims. Is there any definite "pattern" either way?

Secret Saucer Conquest

Those who believe the UFO's are not friendly to us, and may even be secretly surveying earth for their "D-Day," cite several factors as indications of their nefarious intent.

A) *Radiation burns* that various people have suffered from the near presence of UFO's, of which the Itaipu Fort case is the most notorious (Chapter 7).

However, these cases are relatively rare and constitute no direct "attack" made by saucers. They seem to be merely unfortunate side effects when saucers unwittingly sailed or landed close to people. There is no conclusive evidence that the UFO's ever aimed a "burn-ray" deliberately at anyone. The burn effects are probably a byproduct of their electromagnetic propulsion system (Chapter 5).

Thus, accusing them of endangering human life would be quite like a person standing in the engine blast of a jet airliner about to take-off and accusing the pilot of an "attack" on him.

B) *Plane crashes* in connection with sighted UFO's is another point brought up. The following cases are often listed, led off by the most famous one of all:

——January 7, 1948, Godman AFB, Kentucky. When a UFO was spotted by radar, three airborne jet fighters were vectored in toward the object. Two of them gave up when their target proved to be above their ceiling of 20,000 feet—that is, their own personal "ceiling," since they had no oxygen masks along. The two planes elected to turn back down, but Captain Mantell, in the third plane, radioed that he would keep going. He soon reported: "I've sighted the thing. It looks metallic and is tremendous!" Soon after there was radio silence from Mantell, and hours later they found his smashed plane and broken body in the desert. (The Air Force decided he had blacked out from lack of oxygen, but other investigators think a more sinister event might have happened—the UFO's deliberately ramming the jet.)

———July 1947, Washington State. Captain W.L. Davidson and Lieutenant F.M. Brown, two USAF intelligence officers, crashed in their plane after investigating the famed Maury Island case, apparently to find it a hoax. (The opposition hints that the two men did not find it a hoax, and "knew too much" for the secret UFO plans and hence were killed off.)

———January 1956. Colonel Lee Marker crashed as he attempted to pursue a UFO.

———April 1, 1959, near Sumner, Washington. Four people died in the crash of an Air Force C-118 after the pilot had radioed: "We've hit something or *something has hit us!*"

The hostile-UFO adherents believe that that "something" was a UFO, though whether it deliberately rammed the plane or whether it was an accidental collision, nobody can say. It seems rather flimsy evidence that it was a deliberate UFO "attack." After all, with the thousands of UFO's being reported yearly around the world, it would be a wonder, indeed, if a plane and a UFO did not collide occasionally quite by chance.

Time and again, reports tell of UFO's rushing straight at a plane as if to collide, only to make a sharp turn at the last second. Apparently even the UFOnauts at times have difficulty avoiding midair collisions because of their enormous velocity.

UFO Captors

C) *Vanishing planes.* This is a variant of the above category, in which planes vanish without a trace, as if "captured" whole by the UFO's. There are some outstanding and inexplicable cases:

———December 5, 1945, Fort Lauderdale Naval Air Station. A squadron of 5 TBM Avengers went out over the Atlantic on a routine patrol flight. Hours later the flight leader said they were "lost." A huge Martin Mariner was sent to the rescue but also disappeared. All the planes carried life jackets and self-inflating rubber rafts. Yet no trace of the 6 planes or the 27 men ever turned up, though the Navy carried on a three-day hunt with 20 search planes.

The LUFORO BULLETIN (September-October 1952) lists 15 other missing planes from 1913 to 1950, which also vanished without a trace—mysteries unexplained to this day.

The hostile-UFO camp believes that UFO's "capture" these aircraft, probably without damage and with their crewmen alive, for purposes of closely examining our planes and their human pilots.

In keeping with this theory, the many vanishing ships at sea are the handiwork of UFO captors, not to mention the thousands of people who have disappeared from the face of the earth. It all could be true, of course—or false. Very little concrete data or clues have been offered to substantiate this alleged "cabal" devised by the UFO's—except for one remarkable sighting:

——March 5, 1955, Paris, Illinois. Eugene Metcalf witnessed a so-called "plane-napping." A jet plane was pursued by a huge, bell-shaped UFO and literally "swallowed up" by it, seemingly as if a big hatchway had opened and engulfed the plane intact. After churning around in the air, the UFO left, and Metcalf saw no further sign of the plane. (Whether the plane was ever reported missing or not is not stated.)

Saucer Abduction

D) *Kidnapping by UFO's.* Oddly enough, there are several cases of this kind that are seemingly authentic, though they cannot be given an ironclad guarantee as to veracity. Two examples:

——December 25, 1889, near South Bend, Indiana. (A newspaper account unearthed by Frank Edwards.) During a Christmas Eve gathering at a farmhouse 11-year-old Oliver Larch was sent outside to the well to bring in water. A yell was heard—"Help! They've got me!" As the others rushed out they heard only his voice from the sky, growing fainter all the time. Oliver's footprints had stopped abruptly in the snow, his family swore, and the boy was never found again.

——August 20, 1962, Dyas Duas Pontes, Brazil. Raimundo, a 12-year-old boy, swears that his father, Mafra da Silva, was kidnapped in front of his eyes when two glowing UFO's landed near them. They rolled slowly toward the father and emitted a yellow smoke that swallowed him up. When the UFO's sped away, the boy found his father gone.

In the latter case the boy was interrogated by UFO experts in South America, but they could not shake his story. And his father remains missing to this date.

We saw in the last two chapters several cases where saucerians had stolen, or tried to seize, dogs and other animals, as well as human beings. There is a possibility that the UFO's do at times capture earthly people and animals (note the Barney and Betty Hill incident in the preceding chapter) for purposes of examination.

But this hardly constitutes worldwide "aggression" against us, and on the other hand more strongly indicates *scientific interest*. Our astronauts, too, will to bring back specimens of animal life—if it exists—on Mars or Venus when expeditions reach there.

Fireball "Weapon"

E) *Green Fireballs*. This is a special class of "UFO's" whose puzzling nature has never been determined but which seems part of the saucer phenomena.

Starting in November of 1948, strange green "fireballs" were seen streaking across the skies, mostly over New Mexico, Arizona, and Nevada. Too slow to be meteors, too fast to be jets, they were some kind of UFO, particularly because they sometimes changed course or slowed down.

Noting that our White Sands Missile Proving Grounds and our Los Alamos atomic installations—both top secret projects—were located there and were often overflown by the fireballs, the government was concerned about them and put Dr. Lincoln la Paz, foremost expert on meteors, on the job to ferret out the mystery. He has not done so to date beyond stating they definitely cannot be meteors, comets, or any known meteorological phenomena, and look like "controlled" objects.

Some UFO investigators have advanced the theory that the green fireballs represent a "missile weapon" of the saucerians, which they are testing out over the vast isolated deserts of the Southwest—the exact same reason we test missile and nuclear devices there.

However, the green fireballs have yet to strike any target, either in the air or on the ground. On the contrary, they either explode in the air harmlessly or fade out and vanish from sight. Some other explanation will have to be offered to account for these puzzling factors relating to the green fireballs. As proof of UFO hostility, they are a very weak argument.

UFO Earth Survey

F) *Orthotenic earth survey.* This refers to *orthoteny,* a term coined by Aimé Michel in France for his "straight-line" theory of UFO flights. When Michel marked down all sightings on any certain day on a map of France, he was struck by the fact that they often fell into a *straight line,* sometimes across France and into neighboring countries. Also, at certain places there would be a "focal point" where the straight lines crossed, and invariably giant mother-ship cigars had been sighted there.

His supposition was that the mother ships were sent to certain strategic spots to release their "scout ships," which would then make radial flights like the spokes of a wheel.

Some UFO researchers, notably Jacques Vallee, seriously doubt the validity of orthoteny because experiments with beads thrown on any map would often result in the same straight-line and radial geometric patterns purely by chance. Still, Dr. Vallee and other critics do not make an outright condemnation of Michel's theory, which may still

Four glowing UFOs above Naval Air Station, Salem, Massachusetts. Taken by Shell Alpart. *Considered authentic.*

prove correct, or have some other hidden meaning behind it not yet discovered.

Michel's calculations went further and seemed to show that the mother ship positions were always on a *great circle* of earth, which would indicate that it was a *worldwide* UFO survey of our planet, perhaps a systematic mapping in detail of every square inch.

Dr. James McDonald (physicist and Professor of Meteorology at the University of Arizona) has similar views and recently stated: "There are certain patterns that suggest that they (the UFO's) are engaged in something of the nature of reconnaissance. I regard this as the Number One problem before science. It's a problem demanding truly international investigation."

This has led to a listing of where the most frequent U.S. sightings of UFO's occurred:

1. The U.S. atomic energy installations, particularly Los Alamos.
2. U.S. Air Force bases throughout the country.
3. Naval and Marine bases (even those around the world).

4. White Sands missile range in New Mexico.

5. Aircraft plants wherever the industry is most heavily concentrated.

6. Most of America's major cities.

UFOlogists find it significant that the city most "surveyed" was Washington, D.C., the capital of our country, what with some 67 UFO's buzzing over the city in 1952.

We can surmise that the Russians' key bases, installations, cities, and such have also been minutely "scouted" by a kind of "Project Earth Reconnaissance" of the UFO's.

The purpose? The evidence is not conclusive, but obviously one purpose could be the future conquest of earth, once all our defenses and industrial capabilities are thoroughly known to the saucerian warlords.

Yet, an entirely different interpretation can be made of this "orthotenic" survey of earth—that it is merely a peaceful exploration of our world for scientific purposes, just as we map and explore jungles and deserts without any war intent.

Another photo by a government employee, this one over Holloman AFB, New Mexico. Photo copyright by Aerial Research Phenomena Organization.

It depends on how one wants to add up the meaning of the enigmatic activities of the world-ranging UFO's. The following authorities have made a choice and have warned:

—"Our next war will be an interplanetary one. The nations of the world will have to unite against attack by people from other planets." General Douglas MacArthur, 1955.

—"Earth is already engaged in interplanetary warfare, and we are on the defensive." Leonard H. Stringfield, long-known expert in UFOlogy.

—Dr. Olavo Fontes, head of most UFOlogy activities in South America, has also stated many times his considered belief that all UFO activities are the prelude to conquest of earth, once the saucerians are sure of victory.

Peaceful Saucers

In rebuttal to this, the peaceful-UFO camp cites the following general points:

A) To date, no death can be directly attributed to a UFO as a *deliberate* action.

B) The saucers have gone out of their way to observe us without interfering with our affairs or causing any disturbances.

C) Though fired upon by Air Force planes, they have never been known in any documented report to have fired back.

D) The majority of "little men" seen outside of landed saucers have been gathering soil, stones, plants, and perhaps insects—quite like scientists gathering the oddities of a new world.

E) At any rate, being vastly superior to us in flying technology, they could have easily invaded earth years ago, whereas for 20 years they have made no concerted hostile move.

Crashed UFO's

Another dismaying facet to the question of UFO's

being friend or foe is that if we left it up to the Air Force, they would most certainly be our "foes." As mentioned before, it is common knowledge, though officially denied, that for years the USAF has ordered its fighters to fire at UFO's or try to force them down.

There is no authenticated case of any saucer's ever having been damaged or forced to land or crash. The only reports of UFO's crashing are because of internal troubles of their own, perhaps engine failure, sending them to doom.

Most notable is Frank Scully's claims in his 1950 book, *Behind the Flying Saucers*. Briefly, according to a mysterious scientist, Dr. "Gee," three saucers had developed propulsion troubles and crashed near Aztec, Mexico. Within were found the charred bodies of 34 little men, about 3 feet tall, evidently incinerated by the heating up of their craft during the steep plunge.

This tale has been generally discredited, but others sprang up anew, as follows:

———September 14, 1957, Ubatuba, Argentina. Witnesses reported seeing a disc gyrate over the water's edge, then explode in the air and shower down flaming fragments. Some of the fragments were rescued from shallow water and subjected to chemical analysis, but the results have been obscure.

———1952, Spitzbergen Island. A Norwegian flyer purportedly came upon wreckage that was later declared, apparently by Norwegian authorities, to be a flying saucer from another world. But analysis of the wreckage was never revealed, and it was never known if the find was real or not.

———October 31, 1963, near Iguape, Brazil. A young girl was terrified to see a 25-foot silvery disc coming down and striking a palm tree, after which it fell into the Peropava River. The girl called others there, who saw the water boiling violently. In the following weeks various swimmers, scuba divers, and even a man in a diving suit attempted to find the submerged UFO, but the bottom of the river was too muddy to work through, and the saucer was never found.

Dead Saucerians

Perhaps the most sensational claim was that of the 1955 reports from Norway and Germany:

A disc about 100 feet wide was found partly submerged on the North Sea coast of Germany. The object was hauled to Helgoland, a small island, where scientists opened it to find seven dead saucerians, quite human in size and physique, who were badly burned. Maps, books, and various other artifacts were allegedly found.

Matching the above is the news story written by the late Broadway columnist Dorothy Kilgallen, during a visit to England in May 1955:

"I can report today on a story which is positively spooky, not to mention chilling.

"British scientists and airmen, after examining the wreckage of one mysterious flying ship, are convinced that these strange aerial objects are . . . actual flying saucers which originated on another planet.

"The source of my information is a British official of Cabinet rank, who prefers to remain unidentified— 'We believe . . . that the saucers were staffed by small men, probably under 4 feet tall.' "

Friendly Visitors

There are constant rumors and "tip-offs" that pieces of wrecked saucers, or instruments from UFO's, or the bodies of dead saucermen, are held in secret by the Air Force or other government agencies. It might be so. Who knows?

But none of these UFO crashes, if they occurred, was the result of our jet planes' shooting them down. Hostilities have not yet broken open between the saucer-craft and our aircraft. Or at least only one-way "hostility" has been displayed—by our jets. The saucerians simply disdain shooting back, apparently "invulnerable" to our weapons.

Friend or foe? We still don't know the answer. One can only say that on the surface the weight of evidence is against the UFO's planning hostility of any sort, judging by the unobtrusive and "considerate" way they have kept out of our way. In fact, they have done such a thorough job of not "inconveniencing" us or "shoving themselves forward" that their very existence is in question. This book would not have been written if the UFOnauts had been a bit more "forward."

At any rate, this time we have a negative "pattern" regarding the saucers—that they are probably not hostile and plan no secret takeover of our planet.

CHAPTER 14

Unidentified Origin

"Another civilian pilot and myself caught sight of it (a plunging craft) at somewhere between six thousand and seven thousand feet and mistook it for the fuselage of a DC-six airliner in serious trouble, heading for disaster. . . .

"A split-second later it was just about eye-level, and now with great relief we could see clearly it had no wings or appendages of any sort, and no markings or portholes. It was definitely a UFO!

"As the big splashdown came, I turned slightly to observe reactions (of other bathers at the Portsmouth, N.H., beach). . . . I turned back to scan the water just slightly south of the impact point . . . and almost before the spray had settled back on the ocean, the craft shot straight up out of the ocean in a reverse terminal-velocity about a hundred fifty feet or so above the water, dive, flipped over at a perfect ninety-degree angle and flew off without the slightest reduction of speed. . . ."

(Account undated, given by K. Dorn, Shirley, Long Island, New York, as reported in *The Flying Saucer Story* by Brinsley le Poer Trench.)

Do THE UFO'S come from some hidden civilization deep beneath our oceans at the seabottom? This is one of the various theories on the *origin* of the saucers.

Many other UFO's have been seen diving down into or coming up from the surface of the sea. Considering the fact that the oceans cover some 71% of the earth's surface area and that relatively few ships and transoceanic airliners cross those vast expanses, we could assume that more saucers "land" in the sea than on all solid ground in the world put together.

Certain it is that we cannot reject the possible significance of the many sightings of UFO's entering or leaving he sea, and the reports go way back in ships' logs:

———June 18, 1845, aboard the brig *Victoria* off the island of Malta. The crew observed three luminous bodies rise out of the sea about a half mile from the ship and watched them for about 10 minutes.

———May 15, 1879, aboard *HMS Vulture,* on a cruise Commander Pringle reported what appeared to be two revolving "wheels of light," complete with luminous spokes, just below the surface. Amazingly, they took up positions on either side of the ship and accompanied it for half an hour.

(From *The Flying Saucer Story* by Trench)

Similar reports of "glowing wheels" have come from a surprising number of ships, sailing in such varied waters as the Persian Gulf, the China Sea, and throughout the Pacific Ocean. But other types of marine UFO's have been reported also, in modern times:

———June 3, 1961, Savona, Italy. Going offshore quite a way in a motorboat, two men saw the surface of the sea "bulging" a half mile away. Then a disc-UFO with a "cone" on top rose out of the water, shed droplets for a moment, then sped off through the air.

———April 19, 1957, aboard a Japanese fishing boat south of Yokohama. The crew witnessed two discs diving into the sea and leaving a violent turbulence in the water, but no wreckage was found, so it was presumed the saucers had not crashed but had purposely flown underwater.

———September 1, 1957, Porthcawl, Wales. Two shore policemen noticed a glowing, bright red object, with a black zigzag streak across its center, rising up out of the channel waters.

These "amphibious" flying machines, equally at home in the air or in the water, do not necessarily mean they come from a seabottom civilization. The saucers, coming to earth from another world, might simply have chosen the isolated sea depths as their "base" from which to operate. They might, in fact, have merely descended to an underwater cave system of some sunken island or mountain not too far below the surface.

Knowing anything about earthly civilization, the sauce
rians would be well aware that exploration of "inner
space"—the sea, that is—is far behind our current explo
rations of outer space. We actually know less about the
Atlantic Ocean's bottom than we do about the bottoms o
lunar craters.

However, this is only one of many theories, and the
ocean-origin hypothesis has a small following among
UFOlogists.

Other Origins

The list ahead gives the wide range of possibilities of
where the UFO's come from, each no more fantastic than
the other, and none with any strong or definable "pattern" to lift it above the others:

A) *Hollow earth.* This idea has been particularly es-
poused by Richard S. Shaver, one-time writer of the
well-known *dero* stories of underground beings, in *Amazing Stories.* Editor Raymond A. Palmer backed up Shaver's theories and still maintains that the UFO's come
from earth, but he has shifted their home grounds from
subterranean earth to the high atmosphere around it (see
ahead).

The Pellucidar-like supposition, with its assumed advanced culture deep within earth, has as few adherents as
the ocean-bottom theory.

Radiant Beings

B) *Space surrounding earth.* This is Ray Palmer's new
concept, as well as that of others before and after him—
that up in the "radiant" ionosphere, where the Van Allen
Belt holds sway (1,200 to 40,000 miles high) exists some
kind of nonmaterial "energy" civilization of intelligent
beings, invisible to earthly eyes except under special conditions. These radiant creatures occasionally foray down
toward earth's surface, becoming visible in the ionosphere
because of electrical or electromagnetic interactions. Perhaps, the reasoning goes, they are driven down into the
sheltering atmosphere by "space storms" and "solar hur-

icanes" of protons and electrons hurled out by the sun periodically—perfectly valid phenomena hitherto revealed by our space probes.

Palmer pictures a vast and varied "civilization" of the radiant beings, who are as adapted to the "vacuum" of space as we are to living at the bottom of the aerial ocean. Like other kinds of pure energy—radio waves, cosmic rays, ultraviolet rays—they are completely invisible to us up in their realm of "empty" space and only manifest as seemingly solid objects when they plunge down into the ionized portion of our upper atmosphere because of "glow" effects.

But none of Palmer's saucers or saucerians are solid, being more like rarefied plasma gases, though they are nonetheless "real" in their own right.

An offshoot of this theory is the following one.

Vacuum Creatures

C) *Space animal life.* Rather than intelligent beings who soar down in radiant UFO craft, they are thought by some UFOlogists to be more like animal life whose species of energy forms inhabit the fringes of earth's atmosphere.

John P. Bessor of Pennsylvania wrote to the Air Force in 1947 to explain UFO's (*Mysterious Fires and Lights* by Vincent H. Gaddis, David McKay, New York City, 1967):

"I contend that the 'flying discs' are a form of space animal, or creature, of a highly attenuated substance, capable of materialization and dematerialization, whose propellant (power of movement) is a form of telekinetic energy. . . .

"If the seas of our earth are swarming with varieties of living things both great and small, is it not logical to assume that the 'sea' of our sky abounds with sundry forms of living things . . . but adaptable to their celestial environment?"

Others took up this idea and elaborated on it, including the Countess Zoe Wassilko-Serecki of Vienna and Ivan T.

Sanderson, noted American zoologist and naturalist. It was pointed out by them that much UFO behavior is peculiarly like that of animals:

—They play tag (erratic sky maneuvers and "dogfights").

—They are inquisitive (following planes, cars, people).

—They appear to "breed" (the *mother* ships may literally care for a brood).

—They have never directly communicated with humans (discounting the unproven contactee claims).

—They travel in "packs" (various saucer waves).

—They come in many "species" (hence the bewildering variety of UFO shapes and sizes).

—They may have multiple "eyes" (mistaken for portholes).

Earthly animals feed on plants, but plants feed in part on pure *solar energy*. Therefore, why could not space creatures feed *directly* on sun energy? The concept is not scientifically impossible or even improbable, and this would give them enormous flying powers, for the sun pours more energy down on earth each second than all our atomic bombs if exploded at once.

And being of a tenuous structure, like "gas bags" of rarefied air and plasma, the space animals could easily "glide" and speed through the atmosphere in silence and turn corners with ease, not being subject to the usual laws of air friction and resistance.

The analogies go on and on, ingeniously fitting the space-beast concept to the UFO's. But this concept becomes lame when trying to cover the many solid and metallic objects seen very clearly at times with rivets and seams, especially those that land and let little men out. Who or what are the little men "inside" the space animal?

It would seem that "B" and "C" should be combined into one space-creature hypothesis, with both intelligent beings and lower animals sharing their energy-filled realm beyond earth's atmosphere.

Despite inconsistencies with actual saucer sightings, certain reports make one pause before condemning the space-creature theory outright, such as the following:

——August 1, 1952, Cincinnati, Ohio. Workers at a GE plant saw a vivid oval shape that suddenly began to "elongate" and pulsate, "looking like a worm squirming." Another witness tried to explain this as an optical illusion distorting the UFO's true form, but nobody was sure which man was right.

——November 25, 1955, Mt. Mestas, California. A state senator observed a UFO shaped like a dirigible or a tapering barrel, with a "tailed" appendage. It appeared to be oddly "jellylike" in texture and had no distinguishable (metallic) features.

There are other cases of UFO's seemingly changing shape as if flexible, expanding or contracting in size, splitting apart like "amoeba cells," or joining together into one smooth mass, and other manifestations that hardly fit rigid mechanical devices. In fact, the anomalous "changing" saucers have baffled UFOlogists continuously when the latter try to consider them mechanical flying machines.

So the idea of living space animals (or beings) has merit and is not too fantastic to explain the UFO's—which are fantastic from the start.

Time Travel

D) *Future Visitors*. Another compelling idea for the origin of UFO's is that our descendants many times removed, from thousands of years in the future, are visiting us in their past in saucer "time machines."

This would tie in admirably with certain saucer phenomena—their evanescence in general, their "fade-in/fade-out" phases, their sudden, eerie vanishments, their oftentimes insubstantial and even "transparent" texture.

It would also superbly cover the fact that the saucerians do not contact us, for they *can't* under this theory, being from a different "time zone" and therefore not really existing in our time as solid persons or machines, merely as "projections" across the time barrier.

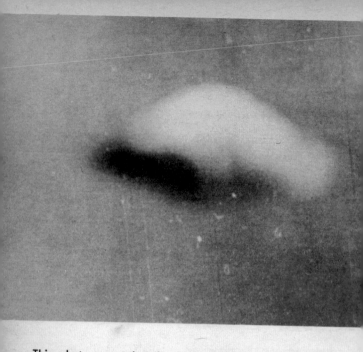

This photo was taken by Ralph Nicholson as he attempted to shoot Sputnik-2, shortly after its launch in 1957.

It is a very intriguing thought, just as if we invented time saucers and then flew back across the time barrier to the early days of Egypt, Greece, and Rome, to thrill at seeing firsthand the dawn of civilization and the great men of those times.

If time travel is possible at all, this UFO origin theory seems quite tenable, even to the extent of explaining the "little men." Evolution will supposedly shrink the human race in time into small, wizened dwarfs with big heads and toothless, slitlike mouths (which are often mentioned in the small-humanoid landing reports).

One can only pass upon this concept of future people visiting their past—and all past eras back to Biblical times or more, apparently—by admitting its engaging logic. In the absence of any proof otherwise, the futuristic concept must be accepted as a contender in the "origin contest."

Colonial Earth

E) *Earth colonists.* This is another thought-provoking and revolutionary theory of grand scope—that ages ago a race of outer space humanoids came to earth to start a *colony* here, just as the early settlers of America planted colonies at Jamestown and elsewhere.

The space colonists either left a band of purebred saucerians—who were quite human and in fact our ancestors—or perhaps interbred with an indigenous man-ape species to create a new hybrid race adapted to earthly conditions.

Then, the supposition is that a worldwide catastrophe or two—such as Noah's flood or the Ice Ages—in the past million years or so destroyed their civilization, wiped out all original records or memories of their true origin, and reduced the colony to a primitive state.

The proponents of this theory have tried to tie in many past-age "mysteries," such as where the amazing Easter Island statuary came from, as well as other remarkable structures that seem beyond the powers of prehistoric cavemen as we vision them.

Also certain very ancient engravings in stone seem to show what look like "saucers" and even men in "diving suits," plus enigmatic writings that have never been translated, as if they are of a nonearthly system of language. Added to this is the fact that many hoary legends, among ancient tribes and empires all around earth, speak of "gods descending from the sky" and aiding mankind with great "magic" powers.

One rather startling bit of evidence is brought up by the earth-colony proponents—the famed Piri Reis map, which shows not only the details of the main continents but also Antarctica. Yet, the map was first known in the early 16th century, long before Antarctica was discovered in 1840.

Researchers claim that the map was actually copied from earlier geographic charts over 5,000 years old, and that such detailed maps that long ago meant that UFO's had cruised over earth in those early days to survey it thoroughly.

Whether that assumption is right or not, the Piri Reis map is genuine and remains a puzzle to this day.

The presence of UFO's today, of course, would then be quite logical, with the parent race visiting and watching the progress of their fallen colony from prehistoric savagery into the age of space and science. Perhaps soon will come the day they can announce what they are and we are, but only when we can accept being a "colony" without rejection of this overwhelming revelation.

Again, nothing positive can be said against this concept, nor has any acceptable proof yet come forth to support this contention. It remains a dark horse in the running for the "origin prize."

UFO Phantoms

There are two more major hypotheses to examine. But first we'll go into one certain UFO "pattern" that could make both concepts viable. It might be called the *fade-in/fade-out pattern*.

In numbers too great to be ignored, many UFO's are reported not to fly away but simply to "fade away" and also to "materialize" before the eyes from thin air, as in the following cases:

——Winter 1952, near Stockholm, Sweden. Six witnesses saw a disc-shaped object about the size of the full moon. As it sped over fields it slowly disappeared in a strange way. "It just went out," one girl said, insisting it was not like an object vanishing in the distance but more like a light being turned off.

——September 8, 1958, Offutt AFB, Nebraska. A group of military personnel caught sight of a cigarlike UFO, surrounded by tiny black specks, and "as it continued on its westerly path . . . it never did drop below the horizon—just faded away."

——December 24, 1960, near Durango, Colorado. A family on a ranch saw a disc with a big dome on top, which remained stationary above them for 15 minutes. Then its glow brightened, turned light green, and finally "faded out slowly, like a gas flame."

Now, it is possible that these UFO's faded out because of flying through a deepening haze in the distance, but the witnesses stubbornly insisted that the objects did not *decrease in diameter* and hence were not moving away as they "faded" from sight.

There may be something deeper to this phenomenon than we suspect.

Cloud-Wreathed Cigars

Even more significant, and very widely reported, are the "cloud cigars" as named by Aimé Michel, meaning the giant cylindrical UFO's that act as mother ships and are often associated with a strange cloudy "mist" or "smoke." Many sightings of these start out with the words: "I was watching an odd-looking cloud when I noticed it began to act peculiar and assumed a regular shape like a cigar." The following instances indicate the ubiquitousness of this phenomenon:

——August 19, 1959, Trenton, New Jersey. The witness saw an object like an elongated cigar, very bright, surrounded by a bluish green haze with orange in the center. During the first 25 minutes of observation it made 8 or 10 right-angle turns. Later five shining objects flew around the cigar; then they all vanished to the northeast.

——October 17 and 27, 1952. The famed Oloron cigar (Chapter 2) was first seen as "a cottony cloud of strange shape," while the Gaillac cigar (presumably the same one) was described as "a plumed cylinder" puffing out smoke.

——September 14, 1954, Vendée, France. A farmer and his hired hands looked up at a thick layer of what looked like storm clouds, to suddenly discern a patch of blue-violet luminous mist in the shape of a "cigar or carrot." The eyewitness account continues: "The luminous cloud appeared rigid . . . and its movements had no connection with the movement of the clouds themselves . . . as if it were actually some gigantic machine surrounded by mists. It came down . . . to an altitude which we thought was perhaps half a mile above us Then it stopped, and the point rose quickly until the object was in a vertical position, where it became motionless."

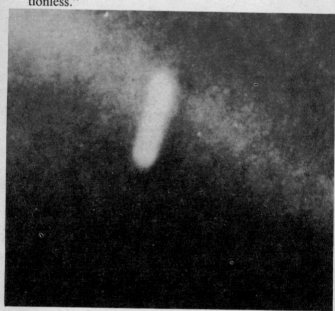

Japanese cameraman Shinichi Takeda took this and other views of a UFO. Seen by many witnesses.

————September 8, 1958, Offutt AFB, Nebraska. This sighting, mentioned before, contains a significant eyewitness statement: ". . . the glow was now diminishing and changing to a dull orange, and at the same time the fuzzy appearance gradually took on a solid look, in the distinct shape of a pencil or slender cigar." It later turned from a horizontal position to an almost vertical position, whereupon the swarm of "black specks" emerged from it.

Note in all of the above cases that the huge UFO-cigar, when stationary, hung either at a vertical angle or straight upright, which is repeated so often in cigar-type sightings that it is definitely a characteristic *pattern* of their behavior.

Now for the significance in the "materialization" pattern, as applied to two origin theories.

Dimension Saucers

The above two phenomena—of saucers that "fade" from sight and the cloud-wrapped cigars that seemingly form out of mists—can both be interpreted as a physical object "materializing" and later "dematerializing" in the earth's skies, rather than "flying" here from some remote point in the universe.

This basic premise leads to the first of two final origin concepts for UFO's:

F) *Dimension ferries*. That is, the idea that beings and their ships are not from another universe but from another *dimension*. Call it a "parallel world" or a "planet from dimension X," presumably from the 4th dimension or beyond. This, too, like the time-travel theory, would specifically account for the UFO's being such elusive phantoms when it comes to seeing, photographing, pursuing, or capturing them.

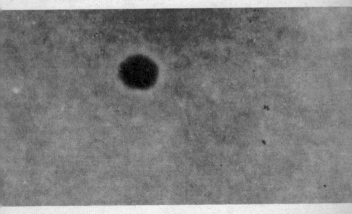

One of the frames from a roll of movie film taken by Al Hixenbaugh of Louisville, Kentucky, June 1950.

As concisely summed up in *From Other Worlds,* a booklet issued in 1964 by Henry R. Gallant and Timothy G. Beckley:

"The UFO's and related phenomena may come from a world having an octave higher degree of vibration in relation to ours. This could be very possible indeed, involving the concept of "worlds within worlds," one interpenetrating the other.

"In reality, we do see and hear within a very limited range and this range can be extended at present with known scientific instruments which scientists and laymen use and experiment with.

"We do not see X-rays, gamma rays, beta rays, radio or TV waves, yet they are all there at the same time, occupying (or traversing) the same space (each) in its corresponding vibrational rate. Similarly, ultrasonics is used for cooking, cleaning, therapy, and cutting heavy steel plates but we are not (aware) and cannot hear it the least bit."

This eerie unseen universe right at our elbow, among the onion-skin layers of interpenetrating universes, is given some support by certain weird sightings (*Flying Saucers* magazine, May 1966, Amherst Press, Ray Palmer Publications):

——In 1944, during an Allied bombing raid on Schweinfurt, Germany, a cluster of small 3-inch discs (foo-fighters) suddenly closed in on the bombers, alarming the crews. Nothing happened, but the men remained nervous as the silent discs paced them and followed their every move when they tried evasive action. Finally B-17 number O-26 seemed about to collide with a cluster of discs. Desperately the pilot tried to evade an imminent collision but could not turn fast enough. Then came the most astonishing thing, as he reported later at the intelligence briefing. His "right wing went directly *through* (italics supplied) a cluster of discs with absolutely no effect on engines or plane surfaces."

——In 1959 a Russian report states: "One of our pilots flew right *through* (my italics) a giant 'fireball'

UFO. When given a searching examination afterward, neither he nor his machine was found to bear the slightest trace or mark. The 'fireball' had simply expanded, as it were, to let him through. Then it contracted again and flew on as if nothing had happened. (But) while under fire from his (the Russian pilot's) machine gun, the 'fireball' had maneuvered and zigzagged, clearly showing intelligent control (remotely)."

——"In the summer of 1961," states another Soviet report, "over the city of Veronezh, a giant cigar-shaped spacecraft carrier (mother ship) at least 800 meters long (about a half mile) came down to a height of only 2,000 meters (about 1.5 miles) in daylight, and hung there immobile. Thousands saw it and there was tremendous panic. Suddenly, the gigantic UFO began to grow transparent and disappeared completely. . . ."

Like old soldiers, some UFO's seem to fade away rather than fly away. Do they "slip" through some "space warp" into the next nearest universe, perhaps occupying the very same space as ours but utterly intangible to us? Will science fantasy of this sort incredibly turn to fact? Only the UFO's know.

Invulnerable UFO's

The possible nonmaterial makeup of the UFO's is given some further credence at another thought. With UFO's constantly flitting through the air, violating landing and takeoff patterns of our own aircraft, one would expect a certain percentage of collisions by now, despite the amazing maneuvers displayed by saucers.

But the seeming absence of such aerial smashups—and claimed cases such as Mantell's death are purely conjectured without any eyewitnesses—could conceivably mean that collisions are impossible because the UFO's have no "substance." They are like "ghosts" in our dimension, as we would be in theirs.

Another eerie aspect of the UFO's is that they can never be shot down, even when seemingly hit. There is a well-documented case that occurred in the U.S. during World War II:

February 25, 1942, Los Angeles, California. Imbued with war jitters, all the city was alarmed as a group of round UFO's suddenly gleamed in the night sky.

Searchlights stabbed into the dark and pinpointed several of the unknowns, and at least one good photograph was taken, which was reprinted in all the nation's press and is still available today.

Antiaircraft batteries opened fire, and exactly 1,430 rounds of ammunition poured into the sky directly at their targets. Gunners swore they had dead aim on the stationary objects, which hung there like "sitting ducks." They had made, they claimed, unmistakable direct hits, many times.

Yet blandly, imperturbably, the UFO's continued to hover, ignoring the bursting flak, exploding bombs, and high-powered bullets. They were absolutely invulnerable, almost as if they were "phantoms" impervious to the material weaponry of earth.

This story has been repeated several times in other incidents, both in wartime and later during the great "saucer hunt" conducted by the Air Force, which had given their jet pilots orders to shoot at the saucers. Never was one damaged or brought down, as far as any unclassified records show.

One thing could easily and logically make them invulnerable—if they were the intangible "dimension craft" of a parallel universe.

We will leave the dimension theory where it is and go on to the one preferred by the majority of UFOlogists as well as scientists.

Extraterrestrial Spacecraft

G) *Interstellar visitors.* One scientist put it that considering the UFO's to be star-ships from a remote galactic world is the "least unsatisfactory solution" to the enigma.

Professor Hermann Oberth, in particular (space rocket pioneer), has staunchly adhered to the other-world concept for years, even speculating that two nearby stars are likely sources for the saucerians—Tau Ceti and Espilon Eridani, both some 11 light-years from earth (very close by astronomical standards).

Oddly enough, after Betty and Barney Hill told their

amazing "abduction" story under hypnosis (*The Interrupted Journey*), Betty drew a "star map" from memory that she allegedly saw aboard the alien ship. It included two stars where the home-worlds of their abductors existed. When this was compared to a real star map, it was found to fit with remarkable closeness the positions of Tau Ceti and Epsilon Eridani. The coincidence seems extraordinary.

But trying to pin down just *which* star system (or systems) the UFO's come from is immaterial at present. The interstellar theory merely says that they come from *some* star and its planets, near or far away.

The supreme logicality of this concept is strongly buttressed by current astronomical theory as per the following points:

—Astronomers almost unanimously agree that there must be from 100 thousand to 100 million habitable planest in our Milky Way Galaxy alone.

—Based on the estimated age of the universe, and earth's age, at least half and probably a higher percentage of those worlds—if they bear civilization—would have a more advanced technology.

—It is entirely conceivable that some of those outer space people have had 100,000 or even a million years of marching science, easily allowing for the invention of their fantastically performing craft, including ships that can cross interstellar space from star to star.

—It is also quite possible that they have achieved speeds faster than light (186,300 miles per second), relativity to the contrary, so that they need not spend lifetimes traveling to earth but perhaps make a 100-light-year trip in 100 days, for all we know.

Interdimensional Doorway

It is quite possible, too, that they use a dimensional "shortcut," the same fade-in/fade-out means of materializing on earth as utilized in the preceding origin theory.

But instead of being from another parallel dimension world, forever intangible and "unreal" to us, they would be solid, flesh-and-blood humanoids from the same physical universe that holds earth.

One scientist, at least, (who prefers to remain anonymous), considers this manipulation of dimensional techniques possible and wrote as follows to this writer:

"Consider all the well-documented sightings of objects which appear or disappear *suddenly* (his italics), or change shape. Also the type II phenomena (mother ships) with the materialization of the craft inside a luminous cloud . . . and the cases where an object was seen to *'vanish'* suddenly.

"We should pay special attention to such cases. They may give us a hint for a breakthrough in physics. Everything seems to work as if these observers (of UFO's) had seen successive projections (in our usual 3-dimensional space) of objects of higher dimensionality. This is not incompatible with the idea of either space-travel or time-travel, but it adds a new element—the indication that, by a study of UFO reports, considerable insight could be gained into the nature of our environment, perhaps leading to a revision of our notions of space and time."

This would mean a strange sort of interdimensional "transition" from a distant part of the cosmos to earth—in short, a swift new means of space travel that bypasses both time and distance as such, so that instead of taking 10 years or more to reach earth from a planetary system 10 light-years away, the UFO arrives in the wink of an eye via its dimensional pathway.

Pure science fiction perhaps—which has had a habit of coming true more often than uncomfortable scientists care to admit. As one scientist candidly confessed: "In daring new scientific concepts and breakthroughs that become reality in time, the science fiction writer has *consistently* outclassed the scientist."

When Arthur C. Clarke, famed science fact and science fiction writer, first presented his idea for communications satellites in orbit, back in 1945, it was scorned as "tommyrot" by most scientists of the day—those same scientists who today may make transoceanic phone calls to Europe via the Telstar/Syncom radio-relay satellite system of ComSat Corporation.

Thus, this plot-device from science fiction of a "space warp," to easily whisk from one end of the universe to nother, may be plain scientific *fact* to the UFOnauts. This would definitely account for their craft's appearing n such massed numbers around earth, for round trips would be just two winks of an eye, easily allowing them to report back to their home world on earthly doings.

lien Pattern

In this chapter no particular "pattern" has presented itself except perhaps the *pattern of alienness,* wherein no matter which theory of saucer origin is examined, the place they came from is utterly alien, abnormal, unearthly. On this, all the concepts agree.

And in the next chapter we will take up the greatest saucer secret of all—*why they have not contacted us.* An xceptionally provoking pattern, based on the behavior of he UFO's and the UFOnauts, will come forth.

CHAPTER 15

Greatest Saucer Secret

February 3, 1953. "Over Washington, North Carolina," stated Marine pilot Lt. Ed Balocco, "I saw what looked like an airplane with red lights. . . . It moved below me, ten thousand feet vertically, in a matter of seconds."

Startled, he turned to chase the object, and his account continued: "The object was the color of white heat, and it threw a red glow behind it."

The pilot thought he gained on the object for a time but never got closer than within 10 miles after which the UFO abruptly disappeared toward the coast at blazing speed.

IN A PREVIOUS chapter we reviewed certain cases of "curious" saucers and "inquisitive" UFOnauts. But by far the great majority of saucers and operators are notoriously "shy" and seem to be deliberately *avoiding* any close contact with people on earth.

This *shyness pattern* persists even after 20 years of sightings in the U.S. and around the world, for reasons unknown to us. Cases of this type crowd all lists of sightings:

——July 7, 1952, near Washington, D.C. A ball of light approached an airliner, but when the pilot switched on all his cabin lights, the UFO took off at tremendous speed.

——January 28, 1953, near Albany, Georgia. Radar spotted a UFO, and an F-86 was scrambled to intercept it, but the round object immediately sped up and vanished in the distance.

——September 7, 1954, Origny, France. Seeing a disc maneuvering up and down, then hovering low over the ground, a motorist turned his headlights on it, whereupon the UFO took off at terrific velocity.

——November 26, 1954, Millville, New Jersey. A disc with body lights circled the town, but when a searchlight was turned toward it, the UFO shot away.

hy Humanoids

The "little men" who emerge from landed saucers, ostly at night, are equally shy, as in the following cases:

——September 10, 1954, Nord, France. A metal-worker came out of his house to see a dark object parked on the railroad tracks, and two little men were running toward it. When the observer tried to chase them, they shot back a beam of light that "paralyzed" him; then their craft shot into the sky.

——October 11, 1954, Taupignac, France. Three men in a car stopped to investigate a disc that landed in a field. Four little men seemed busy near their saucer, but when they spied the humans, they rushed into their disc, shooting back a blinding beam so that the men could not chase them.

——March 18, 1950, Lago, Argentina. A rancher walked toward a landed disc, in which, through a big "window," he saw four creatures dressed in "cellophane" with very pale faces. Upon spying the rancher, they turned on a blinding searchlight beam and then took off straight up in their machine.

Does this extreme "shyness" mean the saucerians don't want to contact us earth people? If so, *why not?*

That is the greatest secret of all about the elusive UFO's. Why have they been patrolling around earth for 20 years, or perhaps centuries, without attempting to communicate with us to explain what their mission is here on our world?

The anti-UFO contingent has made much of this fact, citing it as "proof" that saucers don't exist at all, otherwise their operators would long ago have revealed themselves openly. This viewpoint may seem hard to refute at first, but, like applying our limited technology to their undreamed-of advances, we are using our limited rationalizations to explain saucerian motives when, in fact, they may think on entirely different levels than we do.

Secondly, the UFO-hostility proponents see the silence of the UFO's as obvious—they don't want to tip off their hand before "U-Day," the day of conquest. However, conquest has been rejected as of low credibility in a previous chapter, so we will pass it by here and go on to other motivations for the saucer peoples' visiting earth.

Silence Solutions

Many UFOlogists and saucer researchers have given their own pet theories or listed various possible answers out of which come the following.

The UFO's maintain silence and avoid contact because:

A) Earth is a "dangerous" world, for after achieving full space travel, it may extend its warlike tendencies out into the universe at large. We are, in effect, being "quarantined" by the UFO's without being told about it.

B) The saucerian race comes from a dying world and is "surveying" earth as a new home planet, planning to migrate here en masse, with or without our consent.

C) An alien "Peace Corps" is planning how to aid our "backward" world but must do it in a secret way, or have not yet completed their master plan for that big task. (Theory by courtesy of Brayce Gembler of New Jersey, private UFO investigator.)

D) The UFOnauts are making a purely scientific study of earth with no intention and no real need to contact us, being just scientists and not ambassadors or sociologists.

E) Carrying the above a step further—the saucerians are so far advanced mentally that no real contact is possible, no more than would be obtained between an entomologist and the ants he studies.

F) The saucerians are deliberately withholding contact, well aware of the dangers of disrupting our civilization and our social fabric by the mind-numbing realization that greatly superior beings exist in the cosmos, making earth a "dumbbell" world.

G) Contact has actually been made—perhaps with the

.N.—but is not to be announced publicly until the
orld has been better prepared for the shock.

arth Quarantine

Taking them up one at a time—is earth under "quar-
ntine"? It would almost seem so if one added up certain
ghtings into a significant pattern, such as:

—The massive concentration (30%) of all U.S.
saucers being sighted in the Southwest over our missile
ranges (White Sands) and atomic installations (Los
Alamos).

—The peculiar fact that massed sightings began in
mid-1947, some two years after earth exploded its first
atomic bomb (and just long enough for craft to arrive
on the long trip from their planet?).

—The fact that *every astronaut* of ours, though not
officially admitted by NASA, has seen UFO's following
him in orbit, from John Glenn's pioneering flight to
the many Gemini missions.

—The strange "coincidence" that UFO's are always
spotted at the scene of a nuclear bomb test (before the
ban on atmospheric testing began).

Apparently the UFOnauts are keeping a strict watch
n our progress both in atomics and in space travel. Some
JFOlogists predict we will meet a shocking surprise when
ve try to land men on the moon, whether Russian or
American—our spacecraft may be stopped on the way
nd forced back by "Space Vigilantes." If true, 1969 or
970 should tell the tale.

Aimé Michel, in his saucer books, has asked his read-
rs to put themselves in the place of the saucerians, as
hey looked down and observed earthly doings for centu-
ies—to see an endless series of wars culminating in the
olood-baths of World Wars I and II; murder and crime
ampant everywhere; famine in the midst of prosperity;
he endless hordes of miserably poor around earth; our
oainful progress toward social reform; and all the rest of
ur inhumane transgressions.

As Aimé Michel sums it up: "Considering our bloo[d]
past, would they not be justified in thinking that their be[st]
protection is an 'iron curtain'? Life on earth seems no[r]
mal to man. But what might an *outsider* think, for exam[m]
ple, of the daily slaughter of millions of domestic anima[ls]
to satisfy our needs (to eat)?" (*From The Truth Abo[ut]
the Flying Saucers.*)

Food for thought, indeed, if the "Space Sheriffs" hav[e]
orders to prevent earthly spacecraft from ever spreadin[g]
to other worlds. We may, in a sense, be an "occupied"
world already, done so subtly and carefully that we a[re]
unaware.

Space Migrants

Taking up point "B," are the desperate saucerian[s]
seeking a new world on which to live, their own being de[-]
stroyed or useless?

Although possible, this premise is rather unsound o[n]
several counts. As analyzed by Justin Case (James Mose[-]
ley's *Book of Saucer News*): "Our visitors would un[-]
doubtedly look very much different than we do (i.e. th[e]
little-men humanoids). They would be subject to suspi[-]
cion, fear and hostility . . . (and) be blamed for all sort[s]
of unfavorable events (if they tried to live with us o[n]
earth)."

Besides, one might conjecture that any race of maste[r]
scientists able to build the mighty space-crossing UFO['s]
would also be able to overcome any threat to or declin[e]
of their presumed "dying world." They could, for in[-]
stance, prevent collision with some wayward planetoid[,]
dig underground if their sun cooled, devise a "refriger[-]
ated" world if the sun grew too hot, etc.

Great world-saving feats of almost any magnitud[e]
should be within the capability of a highly advanced peo[-]
ple using giant forces inconceivable to us.

Thirdly, mass exodus of millions of their people acros[s]
space, requiring a gigantic fleet of spaceships, might b[e]
the one colossal task they could not accomplish. And[,]
fourthly, as Dr. Jacques Vallee points out, they would b[e]
much more likely to choose an *uninhabited* world and us[e]

Young Bert Bula saw three glowing objects over his New Jersey home, ran to get his camera, had time for only one snap before the UFOs vanished.

A controversial, mysterious message left by a spaceman in the hands of John Reeves, Brooksville, Florida, in 1965. Air Force experts claim to have decoded it easily, suspecting hoax, but Reeves claims otherwise.

"Angels," as seen on radarscope. Typical radar sighting. Note circle around one presumed UFO, arrows to two more.

Left: Professor Luther Hawthorne, late astronomer, reported several sightings of objects foreign to earth. Though challenged, he maintained he had seen UFOs. *Right:* Dr. J. Allen Hynek, chairman of the astronomy department of Northwestern University, recently stated, "Science can no longer afford to ignore the UFO phenomenon."

"planetary engineering" to fix it up suitably for living purposes. Why crowd in on a world like earth with billions of natives there already, who one way or another would be a stumbling block?

Galactic Peace Corps

In point "C" we meet the favorite theme of the contactees, most of whom seem to meet "noble" people who proclaim they are here to solve earth's every ill. But one wonders when they are going to get started, for they have certainly not cured one ill yet in 20 long years.

However, aside from the brash contactee claims and preachments, we cannot wholly dismiss the possibility that there might be a galactic-style "United Planets," whose membership is a million delegate worlds, which was organized perhaps 500,000 years ago for the "betterment of the universe."

They just might be playing a United States role in the cosmos, sending their "peace corps" here to first study what ails earth—a task that might well take more than 20 years—and then apply their remedies distilled from far wiser minds than ours.

Astronomers and scientific authorities are not above speculating along these gradiose lines:

—"A central Galactic Information Repository, which keeps tabs on all habitable worlds and watches for the uprise of intelligent beings, might someday welcome earth in the Space Community." Dr. Carl Sagan, head of Astrophysics research, University of California.

—"Earth may someday be invited to join the Interstellar Club of advanced, civilized worlds." Dr. Fred Hoyle, famed international astronomical authority and Professor of Astronomy, Cambridge University, England.

—"A growing number of scientists are now convinced . . . this satellite (a mysterious UFO in orbit in 1962) . . . is a visitor sent by superior beings of a community of other stars within the Milky Way Galaxy—a kind of *United Stellar Organization*." *Newsweek* editorial, after interviewing scientists at the National Space Surveillance Center (Spacetrack).

However, none of them speaks of such planet groups *aiding* earth but merely waiting for us to achieve a high enough level of civilization to meet membership requirements to their assembly. Thus, it is probably just wishful thinking that the UFO "Samaritans" are here to help us "leap ahead" thousands of years, for this might result in chaos on earth. Our minds and scientific insights would be too crude and underdeveloped to understand or appreciate it all. Like people, worlds must "grow up" and mature by themselves, as there is no substitute for painful experience, and no shortcut to mellowed wisdom.

Sadly enough, we had better give up this beautiful dream of "fairy godmothers" from space with a sigh and turn to more logical possibilities to explain the hovering UFO's.

Earth "Anthill"

Point "D"—a scientific study of earth, impersonally—seems logical on the face of it if we make the premise that they avoid, or are "forbidden" to try, interfering with any world's affairs by galactic law.

However, as other UFO writers have pointed out, the strong probability that UFO's have visited earth for ages undermines this theory. The UFO scientists would long ago have exhausted every bit of earth data to catalog.

Only one special kind of study might still rescue the theory—if the UFO's return regularly in "waves" to study *humans* and their always changing society. This might be one of the missions sent forth from the "Intergalactic Institute of Planetary Cultures," for example.

Point "E" is among the more valid suppositions—that the saucerian scientists are too advanced to cross the mental barrier and reach our "low level" intellects. If we shed all our anthropomorphic self-worship and look at it in the light of cold reason, it is quite likely that the UFOnauts are completely *alien* to us—in form, mentality, thinking processes, concepts of "good" and "bad," or any other area of psychic development.

It may, in short, be *impossible* for there to be a meeting

of alien-mind and earth-mind, just as there can be no exchange of thoughts or information between humans and apes. Their "language" would be totally incomprehensible to us, and they in turn might find our "ape" language too primitive to decipher, based on a different process of thinking.

Think of the fact that right here on earth today we have two branch cultures and basic societies—free-enterprise capitalism and Soviet Communism—which are poles apart in understanding and goals. If even two large communities of the human race can be so divergent in their way of thinking, then it is not illogical at all that with saucerian and earthly minds the twain shall never meet.

The UFO-skeptics might cry that this is making a baseless theory fit the facts. Yet the premise has a high possibility with no major flaw to weaken it. Only our self-idolizing provincialism makes us want to people the outside universe with images of ourselves, physically and mentally. The real truth may be an ego-smashing surprise.

World Pandemonium

Point "F" is not the same as "D" in that it is not a scientific aloofness that puts the silence ban on UFO's but a deliberate realization that announcing themselves openly can be disastrous. To earth, that is.

For once that day comes, earth will never be the same. Scientists and other top thinkers on earth would face humiliation before a race of super-Einsteins. Our aircraft industy would no doubt crash immediately in the face of new saucercraft, beside which all our flying machines look like motorized kites.

The stock market, our educational system, our methods of government, our systems of philosophy—almost every institution on earth would face revolutionary new modifications and wholesale changes that could result in pandemonium and a social cataclysm.

There are many examples of this in earth's history, when a lesser culture was confronted by a superior people —notably the American Indian when the European settlers came. And in today's tight, interconnected world the decaying or collapsing process would not take decades or centuries but mere weeks and months.

This leads us into the final point . . .

Hidden Contact

Point "G"—that contact has been made with certain authorities, perhaps the U.N.—could be the actual case, with all the above calamities weighing on the minds of those "in the know."

It is even conceivable that all governments or their heads, from the U.S. President to leaders around the world, have had secret but unmistakable contact with the saucer aliens. The two of them—aliens and earth authorities—may now be trying to solve the intricate problem of how to introduce the other-world people and what they can do for us without disrupting our own world's economy, philosophy, peace of mind, and way of life.

One can just picture our President announcing over TV that an "intergalactic loan" from the saucerians will at one stroke alleviate our urban renewal, air pollution, and traffic problems, under the *supervision* of the space visitors.

The hue and cry would undoubtedly arise: "Those 'monsters' running our affairs?" . . . "Who do they think they are?" . . . "Bet they're coming out ahead somehow" . . . "Go home, alien!" We need not point out how close to home this comes, human nature being what it is. Feelings might run so high, especially if the humanoid little men look "alien" at close range, that riots could result all over earth.

The end result could well be a very sudden alliance of all nations on earth, in spirit or in deed, as the unconscious thought arose: "It's us against the universe." If a saucerian-U.N. contact has been made, they might now be in the throes of forestalling such distorted reactions among mankind with the thought of cooperation or mingling with unearthly or at least nonearthly creatures.

And, in fact, this is the only theory that makes sense out of the U.S. Air Force's ill-disguised "cover-up" of the truth about the UFO's' actual existence, and their often-times inane and blundering attempts to "explain away" saucer sightings. The USAF may be under strict orders not to give away the big news until the U.N. has prepared the world for the stunning announcement—a task that may take years more of study and planning with the aid of the aliens.

This premise makes the assumption that the stellar people are not impossibly "alien" in appearance or mentality but close to human physically and in their thought processes. They might even hope to open up "space commerce" or other profitable enterprises with earth.

There may be, as some UFOlogists like to believe, a "space common market" out there, which various adjacent worlds are invited to join for mutual economic benefits. Earth products might then be shipped to other worlds that can use them, in return for exotic wares to delight and excite our people.

But this again partakes too suspiciously of "extending" something earthly into space—this time our economic system and way of life based in good part on material things and creature comforts.

One can hardly picture our present human ways and systems holding up into the future for 25,000 or 500,000 years on earth, let alone on other worlds. As time passes, civilized societies would undoubtedly evolve through various stages, just as mankind went through Stone Age times, the rise of empires, feudalism, the advent of steam, and the rise of modern science.

The end result, for any far-future time on any world, must surely be something remote to the understanding of the current society, in each case. Commerce, trade, importing and exporting, money, checks, business deals—all such may be only historical memories of things gone by on advanced planets, and on earth of 50,000 A.D.

In fact, one can hardly think of *anything* we have on earth that is likely to interest supercivilized beings who create food, metals, power, and all the necessities with ease. Perhaps only one thing might intrigue them—the chance to study a rising civilization going through its youth pangs. For this, in order to get the fullest possible data, they might have made contact with the authorities secretly. And it might then be that they have promised to leave in due time, in the next century or so, obviating the necessity of upsetting earth by telling the truth publicly.

There are, naturally, many other twists one could give that basic theme and all the other preceding theories as to why, so far, the saucermen have not made contact with us or have done so only guardedly.

Frustrated Contact

One odd theory held by a small group of UFOlogists is that the saucerians have actually been *trying* to make their presence known through the years but have not succeeded. Judging from the obtuseness of the Air Force, one can readily see some merit in this thought. But they cite other points to bolster their concept:

—The fact that millions of worldwide sightings have been made since 1947, which is hardly "hiding" themselves.

—That the plane-pursuers and auto-chasers may be trying to find a "welcome" reception somewhere instead of the universal attempts to shoot them down and people running in fright.

—That the UFOnaut little men, in particular, seem in some cases to be attempting friendly gestures, sign language, even vocal language directed at human observers of their landings.

But these efforts have come to nothing, so far as is known (except for the unacceptable claims of the full-fledged bookwriting contactees).

However, the "silence pattern" is too strong and widespread through the body of sightings for us to believe seriously that the UFO's are attempting to set up communications, which we rebuff or stupidly fail to recognize. Surely a concerted effort at contact by hundreds or thousands of UFOnauts, if they so desired, would reach the people and/or the authorities.

Space Exploration

One other important factor that ought to quiet the UFO skeptics has been left for the last. Let us look over a list of "rules" that space explorers might follow:

—The expedition of several spacecraft, upon reaching target world, will go into orbit and will send down landing craft *only if there are no signs of current civilization below.*

—If it proves there are people on the planet, the first expedition must *return without any landings.*

—A second expedition will then be outfitted with the proper sensors and equipment for *surreptitiously exploring an inhabited planet.* Under this plan great care must be taken to carry out a step-by-step program as follows:

A) Orbital sensors must be set up to *photograph and survey* the planet thoroughly.

B) All *military defenses* of the native people, if any, must be pinpointed.

C) Observations must be made to determine if the natives are in a *less advanced state than earth, or greater.*

D) If the people prove hostile, *great care must be taken when landings are accomplished.*

E) Landings should be made only in *remote areas with sparse population, never in big cities.*

F) Scientific teams should then land and collect *samples of soil, native flora and fauna, and other specimens of interest.*

G) If natives appear near a landed craft, *under no circumstances are they to be fired upon.*

I) Such a landing crew will *leave immediately, taking off into space to the mother ship.*

J) *Strict secrecy about the presence of our spaceships* must be maintained at all costs, so that only night landing flights are safe.

K) *No attempt at direct contact should be made* until and unless a favorable reaction can be expected from the native populace.

L) If the inhabitants seem to be unable to accept the idea of visitors from another world without panic, *contact must be put off indefinitely.*

M) All possible precautions must be used to keep the natives *in doubt as to the reality of the landing craft* that carry on clandestine explorations.

N) The above operations and steps, requiring several expeditions, *may stretch through a lengthy period of years or decades,* with the presence of earthly craft kept secret.

NASA's Project Mars

This is not the author's attempt to fathom the mission "rules" that are obeyed by the UFOnauts.

It happens to be a paraphrased, but accurate, list of rules for a proposed Mars Exploration Mission, as tentatively outlined by NASA, the agency that runs America's space program.

NASA, which officially scorns anything connected with flying saucers, drew up these plans independently, little realizing how remarkably they fitted the very *pattern of exploration* the UFO's seem to be conducting on earth.

This, then, may be the most logical explanation of all for why the UFO's are here and why they don't openly admit it and reveal themselves. They have not yet, we may assume, gathered sufficient data on whether humans are *safe* to deal with or not. It would not be easy, even in 20 years, to analyze fully our complex civilization with its many ramifications, contradictions, and mazes of human endeavor, philosophy, politics, international relations, cultural levels, *et al.*

Our language, for instance, may be a hard nut for them to crack, particularly if they have no vocal cords and converse some other way, such as by vibrations, telepathy, or whatnot.

The paradoxes rife on earth—some nations living in peace while others battle bloodily, poverty next door to plenty, the great variety of military weapons that are little different from space rockets—might stump the UFOnaut experts for a long time before they can unravel the meaning of this strange society and its queer doings.

Twenty years into the mission. Are the saucerians nearing the end of their study when they will decide contact can be made? Or have they already reached the conclusion that our "neurotic" society can *never* be contacted?

So a "NASA" of another world or world-group may have sent out their "Earth Exploration Mission" destined by their rules always to be evanescent phantoms in our skies and a perennial riddle to mankind.

But again, to be objective, this "NASA pattern" may be a false projection of our limited concepts of space exploration into another world's motivations and methods.

Or it may not be.

Sphinx Saucers

Are any of the premises we have reviewed valid? On that, since there isn't the slightest shred of real evidence one way or another, you must decide for yourself. The UFOnaut visitation may be for unfathomable reasons remote from any of those concepts and perhaps beyond the reach of the human mind.

The only thing we are sure of is that there is a *pattern of silent secrecy* on the part of the UFO's for the past 20 years or more. For every UFO that briefly follows a plane or UFOnaut that waves a friendly greeting or saucer that exposes itself openly to the gaze of thousands over a city, there are ten UFO's that dash away from every pursuing jet, avoid any human observer after a landing, and never attempt to signal us in any way.

The *no-contact pattern* must be taken into account in devising or accepting any particular theory of who the mysterious saucerians are and why they are here on earth.

CHAPTER 16

USAF versus UFO's

January 11, 1965, Washington, D.C. Radarmen at the airfield spotted about a dozen UFO's, and the news came to a group of Army communications experts, who dashed to the windows and saw the saucers, which were being chased by Air Force jets.

"They agree on the shape," reported the *Washington Star,* "and approximate number of discs, and the fact that the things were speeding faster than the jet interceptors."

But in an official announcement later, in behalf of the Air Force, the Defense Department stated flatly: "There was no such incident. It just did not happen."

The Army experts are sure it did.

THIS NEATLY SUMS up the official attitude of the United States Air Force regarding UFO's—like the giraffe, there is no such thing.

The USAF has earned for itself the scorn and bitter epithets of almost everyone in America who has sighted a saucer and reported it to them. The luckless observers are met either with the above outright denial of the sighting's having occurred or with ridicule and are handed official "explanations" that often border on the absurd.

For example, during one flap (series of rapid sightings) in Oklahoma in 1965 the Air Force came up with the bland explanation that the objects had really been the stars in Orion's belt, seen under "peculiar atmospheric conditions." This was meant to cover a sighting in which a fleet of UFO's swept across the sky, pausing to perform some aerial gymnastics first.

186

An astonished astronomer hastily checked his star charts, then sadly informed the USAF that the Orion Constellation on that date (and season) was below the horizon and not visible in the northern hemisphere.

Why does the USAF try to discount and discredit all UFO's with single-minded fanaticism—even more fanatically than some UFOlogists claim they are proved to exist? For 20 years, except for a brief period from late 1947 to early 1949, the Air Force and the Pentagon have doggedly pursued this "denial policy." And this in itself becomes one of the strongest *proofs* that UFO's really exist and that the Air Force knows it. The protest-too-much campaign of the USAF seems the classic pattern of covering something up by loudly and persistently trying to claim that it is much ado about nothing.

A "nothing" that the Air Force itself hunts down relentlessly and continuously to this day, contradicting its own statements.

USAF Vacillations

The Air Force was given the task of checking the sudden flood of saucer reports after Kenneth Arnold's historic sighting of June 24, 1947. In July their investigation began under the ATIC (Air Technical Intelligence Command) at Wright-Patterson AFB near Dayton, Ohio. It was first called *Project Sign*.

Soon after, in September 1947, the ATIC announced that the UFO's were real and were probably "interplanetary vehicles." This was the official line until February 11, 1949.

Then abruptly, in one of those bewildering about-faces the ATIC has become noted for, the name of the mission was changed to *Project Grudge,* and its conclusions completely reversed the previous statement and officially denied that UFO's even existed.

This came about, according to Captain Edward J. Ruppelt (*The Report on Unidentified Flying Objects*), because of internal disagreement within the USAF over the significance of the UFO's. By the end of 1949 Project Grudge claimed that all reports to date had been delusions, illusions, mirages, hysteria, hoaxes, and crackpot tales. The project was then abandoned because "there was nothing left to investigate."

Actually, and in complete secrecy, the investigation went on at an increased tempo through 1950 and 1951. Public protests and continuing UFO sightings then forced the USAF to pretend to "revitalize" the already high-gear program, giving it a new name—*Project Blue Book,* the name it is still known by today.

Captain Edward J. Ruppelt was put in charge and for 2-1/2 years did a remarkably good job with his small staff of half a dozen people. He was given authority to ask for saucer reports made to any Air Force base in the country, and they poured in.

Though Captain Ruppelt was forced by his superiors to keep denying that there was any indication that the flying saucers were "real," he was retired in September 1953 and three years later published a book—*The Report on Unidentified Flying Objects*—in which he said he believed that the "hard core" unexplainable cases meant UFO's did exist.

In an ironic statement he said: "What constitutes proof? Does a UFO have to land at the River Entrance to the Pentagon, near the Joint Chiefs of Staff offices? Or is it proof when a ground radar station detects a UFO, sends a jet to intercept it, the jet pilot sees it, and locks on with his radar, only to have the UFO streak away at phenomenal speed? Is it proof when a jet pilot fires at a UFO and sticks to his story even under the threat of court-martial. Does this constitute proof?"

Obviously it does or comes mighty close to it. Ruppelt also revealed the schism within the USAF itself from the first days on. One group, including high Pentagon officers, believed that the UFO's were real and, in fact, were interplanetary spacecraft from another world. Another group remained skeptical of the reality of UFO's entirely, and they won out in fashioning official policy, which from 1949 to date has been never to admit anything positive about UFO's and to imply that they do not exist at all.

The "Silence Group"

Major Donald Keyhoe coined the term "Silence Group" for these anti-UFO Air Force Chiefs. Apparently because the tug-of-war seesawed back and forth between the "tell-all" group and the "tell-nothing" faction, a long series of bewildering and often contradictory pronouncements came from the ATIC—sometimes half confessing that UFO's existed, more often denying it.

In January of 1954 reporters were banned from seeing ATIC reports on saucers and from then on began a concerted effort to suppress all UFO news in order to delude the public into believing that the whole phenomenon had "ceased."

All the while reports kept coming in steadily, making another big jump in 1957, but the Pentagon's Tell-Nothing Group kept the lid on tight. Even the wire services were fooled into considering all foreign saucer reports, which rose to a feverish pitch, as sheer "nonsense" and failed to reveal to the American public that not only had the saucers not vanished, but they were increasing their activity all around earth. The whole worldwide wave of 1954 was ignored.

Pursuing its course with fanatic intensity, the Air Force tried to squelch the truth about UFO's by the following measures:

—It forbade any USAF pilot from revealing his UFO sighting (military pilots accounted for some 17% of all cases) to the public, under threat of court-martial.

—It pressured the airline companies also into silencing their civilian pilots (officially denied, but another 13% cut off).

—It instructed ATIC to release to the public "only those UFO reports in which they are explained *away* as illusions or conventional objects." (Italics supplied.) In short, any *unknown* would never come to public attention.

—It released yearly "Special Reports" by Project Blue Book that purportedly showed that up to 98% of all sightings had been definitely analyzed as illusions, conventional objects, or hoaxes and that the other 2% would probably be explained similarly after more study, implying that there really were no "unknowns" at all.

Paradoxical Policy

Yet all this while, in complete contradiction to its supposed disinterest, the Air Force:

—Sent a private notice on December 24, 1959, to all Air Force bases saying that "UFO's are serious business" and every sighting must be investigated and each UFO must be chased by a jet interceptor if possible.

—In August of 1960, reenforced this with another statement saying that there must be "continued surveillance of the atmosphere near earth for UFO's."

—Rushed Intelligence agents to the scene when any significant sighting was reported, anywhere in the country, with clandestine orders to "ridicule" or otherwise cast doubt on the sighting while at the same time gathering any photographs made. (In many cases these photographs and strips of movie film were *never returned,* or false copies were sent back, according to individual witnesses.)

Following this contradiction, the USAF became entangled in its own web of lies and deceits and coverups so thoroughly that when the 1965-66 "champion" wave came along, its anti-UFO campaign collapsed into rubble.

Soon after, the Air Force announced that it was turning over UFO investigations to a scientific team under Dr. Edward U. Condon of the University of Colorado—a red-faced admission before the whole country that UFO's could not be "laughed off."

USAF Defeat

The 1965-66 wave, with repercussions all over the

world, has changed the picture for the better. Now everyone is skeptical of the USAF and saucer-scoffing scientists rather than of UFO's.

As an example, the *Times-Star* of Alameda, California, on August 10, 1965, ran a scathing editorial titled: "How Many have Anomia in U.S.?"

The article reads, in part: "According to Air Force spokesmen two weeks ago, a powerful assortment of police officials, sheriff's deputies and various other individuals, including even some members of the Air Force itself, were suffering a mild form of *anomia*—the loss of the ability to name an object correctly—as evidenced by their failure to recognize such obviously common things as weather balloons, planets, comets, etc., when they spotted them in the skies. . . . Their error lay in terming them unidentified flying objects, more commonly known as flying saucers.

"Just how the Air Force spokesmen were able to tell that the hundreds of reports of UFO's from an area about as large as Free Europe (during the 8-state multiple sightings from North Dakota down to Texas) were faulty—and especially how they were able to do it within 24 hours . . . ought to rank as one of the most remarkable examples of lightninglike diagnosis of all time.

"However, it now appears that—as countless thousands of well-informed people have suspected for years now—the Air Force spokesmen were wrong. . . ."

To which one might add the pithy comment: If the Air Force persists in naming unexplainable UFO's as planets, weather balloons, and comets, *then who has the anomia?*

Air Force "Myths"

The USAF/ATIC has "cultivated myths," according to the UFOlogists, and foisted them on the American people for 20 years. Saucer believers and particularly NICAP have tried to destroy systematically every one of the myths with documented refutations. The list:

"MYTH"	THE TRUTH
A—That scientists have never seen or reported UFO's.	A partial NICAP list of scientists who have sighted saucers includes Charles H. Otis (biologist), Wells Alan Webb (chemist), Carl A. Mitchell (physicist), Seymour Hess (meteorologist), Ivan T. Sanderson (zoologist), Lee Ball (biochemist), Melvin C. Vagle, Jr. (metallurgist).

Typical scientist sighting, January 30, 1953, as reported by Dr. Wells Alan Webb, research chemist, University of California:

'While looking through the windshield [of his car] the writer noticed a half mile ahead, among a group of steady bright ground lights, there was one light that flickered and danced. . . .

"Suddenly . . . we became aware of the dancing light's rising motion. . . . The author strained at the rear window and watched the light blink repeatedly, then vanish among the stars. . . .

"When all the facts about the light (that) Gelber, Kihorney and the writer had seen were laid before the weatherman, he said that ours might have been a UFO. . . ."

Astronomer Sightings

Myth B—That astronomers have never spied UFO's through their telescopes or with the naked eye.	Several dozen astronomers —and going back at least a century—have given detailed reports of "unknown objects" crossing the moon's disc or a field of stars in a telescope. Modern astronomers who have reported UFO's are: Clyde Tombaugh (discoverer of the planet Pluto), Walter

N. Webb (Hayden Planetarium, Boston), H. Percy Wilkins (British lunar expert), Frank Halstead (Curator, Darling Observatory).

Typical report, by the late Frank Halstead, November 1, 1955, during a train ride across the Mojave Desert, Nevada:

"My wife Ann was sitting next to the window and she called my attention to an object. . . . I realized it could not be a blimp—they are only about two hundred feet long. And this thing was gigantic. It was about eight hundred feet long.

"While we were watching the cigar-shaped thing . . . we noticed that another object had joined it. This second object appeared very suddenly. . . . It was a disc-shaped thing. . . .

"All over the world credible witnesses are reporting experiences similar to mine. Holding these people up to ridicule does not alter the existing facts. The time is long overdue for accepting the presence of these things, whatever they are, and dealing with them and the public on a basis of realism."

UFO's on Radar

Myth C—Radarscope images of UFO's are never detected, proving them nonmaterial phenomena

NICAP lists at least 80 documented cases of radar sightings, many by the USAF itself. Typical examples follow:

——Summer 1948, Goose Bay, Labrador. Both USAF and RCAF radar stations tracked a UFO speeding at 9,000 mph.

——November 6, 1948, Japan. USAF radarscopes tracked two maneuvering UFO's, having an apparent "dogfight," for over an hour.

——March 8, 1950, Dayton, Ohio. Two F-51 pilots saw a "huge and metallic" UFO, which ground radar then picked up as a solid "blip," unmistakably real.

———July 26-27, 1952, during famed "Washington attack." Various USAF and CAA radars picked up a series of 67 UFO's in one night, with 8 to 12 UFO's on one screen at times, fully confirmed by multiple radarscope records for each saucer.

UFO Photos

Myth D—No authentic photographs or movie film of UFO's have ever been submitted and proven genuine.

Listings by NICAP show at least 64 documented photos or movie strips that even the USAF experts could never prove were faked in any way.

Some of the more famous items are the following:

———Paul Trent, McMinnville, Oregon, on May 11, 1950, obtained some of the clearest UFO photos known and pronounced absolutely genuine by many experts. The domed disc hovered around his farm for many minutes, allowing his excited wife to snap the five pictures.

———Nick Mariana, Great Falls, Montana, took 16-mm movie footage in color of two UFO's, on August 15, 1950. According to Mariana, the best frames, showing clearly that they were discs with rotating rims, were found missing from the filmstrip after being "borrowed" and returned by Air Force investigators.

———Carl Hart, Jr. took night movies of the celebrated "Lubbock Lights," a V-formation of large, circular objects that flew over Lubbock, Texas, on August 31, 1950. Experts watching the sequence stated that the formation "shifted position according to a definite pattern," which could only mean intelligently controlled machines.

———Almiro Barauna, official photographer aboard a Brazilian Navy cruiser, snapped 5 sensational pictures of a Saturn-type UFO on January 16, 1958, near Trinidade Island in the South Atlantic. The photos were vouched for as genuine by the Navy Minister of Brazil.

——Warrant Officer D. C. Newhouse, USN, shot 1,200 frames of color movies of a "flock" of UFO's near Tremonton, Utah, on July 2, 1952. His telescopic lens closeups clearly showed flat, circular UFO discs, but his best frames (like Nick Mariana's above) were allegedly confiscated by the USAF and never returned. Attempts by the USAF to declare they were a flock of birds out of focus failed when a top-ranking scientist of the Douglas Aircraft Company said that certain lighting characteristics related to flapping wings were missing, hence they were not birds. No other explanation was ever advanced, and the filmed UFO's remain as true "unknowns" today.

"False" Phenomena

Myth E—That the so-called "electromagnetic effects" of stalled car motors, headlights blacking out, and people "burned" or "paralyzed" by rays are sheer imagination or hysteria.

NICAP lists a minimum of 70 cases, where witness credibility and reputation are unassailable, or are documented. (See cases in previous chapters on EM effects.)

Myth F—That "angel hair" has never yet been definitely tied to a UFO, and is really a wind-blown mass of spider webs in all cases.

Listed by NICAP are over 40 cases, including at least 25 in which UFO's were sighted and seen to release the fluff. Reliable witnesses all reported that the material dissipated quickly, as in the case described below.

August 6, 1961, Meekatharra, Western Australia. Edwin Payne, a sheep-shearing contractor, sighted 12 white-metal discs, which gave off a fine, fibous substance.

The material, which drifted to earth, crumbled in the hands before it could be preserved. Payne described it as a "snowy-white meshlike substance."

A dozen other people witnessed the 12 UFO's flying overhead in pairs, and it was clearly evident that the substance came from them.

Exploding Myths

Myth G—That UFO's are mainly seen in the U.S., which tends to prove they are local phenomena "talked up" so much here that it amounts to national hysteria.

The news services, by deliberately ignoring the many foreign UFO reports that have come in steadily from the start, have also fostered this false belief. UFO researchers have gathered up to 50,000 foreign cases, proving that saucers are seen everywhere in the world with the same general frequency as in the U.S.

Myth H—That the Air Force is "playing fair" with the public and is not suppressing key sightings or attempting to censor any reports.

Certain saucer reporters have presented clear-cut—and never-challenged—charges of the USAF's withholding original reports in their files under "top secret" classification. And that, secondly (as related before), the USAF has "intimidated" its own pilots and airline pilots into not reporting UFO's (30% combined) they see.

By circulating and nourishing these obvious "myths" constantly among the American people, the USAF has unquestionably obscured and distorted the whole UFO picture, probably not for any nefarious purpose. They have simply badly bungled the job for 20 years.

But the USAF is apparently not alone to be blamed.

CIA's Hand

Dr. James McDonald, senior physicist at the Institute of Atmospheric Physics of the University of Arizona, has long been an advocate of UFO's and recently declared that his investigations show that the CIA, in alarm over the big wave of saucers in 1952, imposed upon the Air Force the policy of ridicule and secrecy. This is reported in *The Flying Saucer Menace* by Brad Steiger, with pictures by August C. Roberts, an Award Books Special, Universal Publishing & Distributing Co., New York City, 1967. In the report Dr. McDonald goes on to say that the CIA's reason seems to have been that investigation of sightings "tied up" military communications channels too much and also usurped too much of the time of USAF intelligence officers.

Dr. McDonald believes that the CIA has since then withdrawn from the scene, but by then Air Force policy was so firmly fixed that it could not be changed from its "denial and doubt" pattern.

A sudden turnabout now, like telling the people they (the USAF) were wrong before and that the UFO's really existed, might very well destroy faith in the Air Force or at least arouse a cry for Congressional investigation and the discharge of many high-ranking officers.

So one can see why the USAF is caught in its own trap, even if we can't sympathize with them for their inept and often idiotic handling of what may be the greatest discovery of the century, if not of all time.

Dr. McDonald further stated that out of eight possibilities of what the UFO's are—mass illusions, unknown atmospheric tricks, frauds, etc.—he chooses "extraterrestrial probes," somewhat reluctantly, because that is the "least unsatisfactory" solution.

He adds: "There is strong evidence that these objects are extraterrestrial vehicles. And scientists all over the world had better stop accepting the ridiculous Air Force reports and start investigating the problem themselves, at once. The matter is urgent."

Panic Policy

After the CIA pressure was off, it seems the favorite Air Force "excuse" for keeping up their secrecy policy was that it might "panic" the American public to know the truth about flying saucers.

In France, during the terrific wave and many landings of UFOnauts during 1954, there was no hint of panic whatsoever among the French people, though the whole country buzzed with the fantastic stories. And Dr. Olavo Fontes, Brazilian scientist, has this to say about the reaction in South America during their big waves of 1954, 1957, and 1965:

"There is no flying saucer controversy here. Too many people—thousands—have seen these objects at close range in Brazil over the last sixteen years." He further reported that except for a few villages filled with excitement over some local sighting the people were now used to the phenomena and were faithfully reporting UFO's to the authorities, hoping to clear up the mystery.

That hardly sounds like "panic."

The Air Force, which has never investigated the saucers in a truly scientific manner (as they claim), has little, if any, right to keep the true story from Americans on the basis of "protecting" us from nationwide panic.

But the problem is now compounded, for unfortunately the USAF's policy has wasted 20 years that might have been more wisely used to *prepare* America—and the world—for the UFO revelation, thus forestalling panic.

Perhaps *now* the Air Force has good reason to continue their keep-it-quiet campaign, but only because they themselves set the stage for this two-horned dilemma. They have, in effect, created a fool's paradise in regard to whether or not we are under observation by aliens from outer space.

Paradox Pattern

Oddly enough, the very fact that the USAF publicly intimates that the saucers are illusionary while privately and desperately checking every sighting and sending jets after each UFO certainly must be viewed with suspicion—the suspicion that the USAF *knows that the flying saucers are really up there*.

This *paradoxical pattern* of Air Force policy is, therefore, one of the *strongest* proofs that the UFO's do exist. But, of course, this conclusion comes through only to the minority of us who have researched UFO's thoroughly. The vast public is still blissfully ignorant of the seething turmoil hidden within the area of saucer investigation, and what an explosion may someday be detonated!

Even if it had tried, the USAF could not have better insured that there *will* be panic of some kind the day that the UFO's are officially declared real.

CHAPTER 17

The Patterned Proof

IT SEEMS THAT, like the case of "stones falling from the sky" (meteorites) in the last century, science must once more be told by the laymen that a genuine new phenomenon confronts us that cannot be ignored, wished away, or made to vanish by "authoritative" statements from eminent "experts."

The Air Force and many scientists are experts only in evading the truth and ignoring the evidence of human eyes—millions of pairs of them all over the world.

The word "millions" is not exaggeration. A recent Gallup Poll disclosed the astonishing fact that 5,000,000 Americans believe they have seen a UFO in the period from 1947 to date *(10,000,000 Witnesses Can't be Wrong,* by this writer, *Mechanix Illustrated,* June 1967).

Even if 80% were optical illusions or conventional objects mistaken for saucers, that still leaves 1,000,000 more-or-less genuine sightings in 20 years, or 50,000 annually.

In America alone.

Since the U.S. has about one-tenth of the world's population, and since UFO's visit every part of earth without exception, the worldwide figure then becomes 500,000 saucers each year for 20 years. That comes out to 1,370 per day, or 57 each hour.

Thus, on the average, a UFO is sighted *once every minute* somewhere on earth. In America alone, the figure would be 6 per hour, still an amazing quantity.

But let us be ultraconservative and *eliminate 99.9% of all sightings.* That leaves, out of the original 50 million worldwide sightings since 1947 (extrapolated from the Gallup Poll), some 50,000 "hard core" sightings around the world in 20 years. America's share is then 5,000, from 1947 to date.

Yet the USAF, in 20 years of investigation, only admits to 652 unknowns in the U.S.

In fact, the ATIC/USAF has acknowledged only 11,000 plus sightings since 1947 as "valid," having thrown out all cases with "insufficient data" after judging them by purely arbitrary standards. On top of that, the ATIC/USAF has scared off many people from reporting at all for fear of ridicule. The story has gone around about that.

Obviously the Air Force has *missed* many, many sightings by their restrictive criteria and narrow acceptance of "valid" reports. Captain Ruppelt, chief of Project Blue Book from 1951 to 1953, estimated that some *180,000 U.S. sightings* were made each year, of which the USAF saw only a selective average of less than 1,000—namely, about one half of 1% of all saucer reports in the U.S.

USAF's Half Half-Truths

Following is the official listing of yearly UFO reports as given by the Air Force:

TOTAL UFO SIGHTINGS REPORTED TO U.S. AIR FORCE

Year	Sightings	Unidentified
1947	122	12
1948	156	7
1949	186	22
1950	210	27
1951	169	22
1952	1,501	303
1953	509	42
1954	487	46
1955	545	24
1956	670	14
1957	1,006	14
1958	627	10

1959	....	390	....	12
1960	....	557	....	14
1961	....	591	....	13
1962	....	474	....	15
1963	....	399	....	14
1964	....	562	....	19
1965	....	886	....	16
1966	....	1,060	....	13

	11,207	652

AIR FORCE ANALYSIS OF 1966 UFO SIGHTINGS
(As of December 1, 1966—856 reports)

Astronomical	....	199
Aircraft	....	195
Balloon	....	20
Satellite	....	100
Other	....	71
Insufficient data	....	103
Unidentified	....	13
Pending	....	155

"Pending" usually means "we're stumped, but if we scratch around awhile, we'll come up with some ordinary objects or conditions that will explain them away."

Quite obviously all Air Force figures are, and always have been, doctored to fit their policy. Included in each year's total are only the cases they "accept," while large numbers are discarded as "worthless."

As proof, we can cite that in 1954, during the great worldwide wave, the ATIC admitted receiving *700 reports weekly* in the U.S. alone. If the peak of the wave lasted 6 weeks, that was 4,200 reports. Why did the USAF only list *429 reports* for the whole year of 1954?

And for the NANA wire service (North American Newspaper Alliance) John Keel reported that there had been 10,000 published reports in 1966, in the U.S., out of which the Air Force lists a meager 1,060. This is wryly comparable to the census-takers' skipping 90% of the people in the country and giving the population of the U.S. as 19,000,000 in 1967 instead of 190 million plus.

Captain Ruppelt gave the opinion that the true "unknowns" (unidentified) should be at least 10 times higher than ATIC figures, which would thus have reached a total of 6,520 today instead of 652. The rest have been statistically juggled out of existence, in the Air Force's avowed zeal to reduce the unknowns to an eventual zero.

But the smoke behind all this fire is hiding the truth—that the worried USAF knows that no statistical manipulation can prove the nonexistence of objects that do exist, whether the Air Force likes it or not.

Hard-Core UFO's

Yet it is irrelevant whether there are 6,000 or 600 witnesses involved. In court, it takes only *one* reliable witness to condemn a man. Therefore, if only one UFO sighting is an ironclad, guaranteed report, the whole saucer case is proved at one stroke, without the other 5,999.

There is not only one such ironclad, documented, irrefutable sighting known among UFO researchers but at least 100 and probably more than 1,000. Yet the USAF judge never lets the case go to court for a fair trial by a jury to hear the witnesses out. By proclamation only, the USAF has taken upon itself the kingly powers of declaring that there are no witnesses and no case.

The matter becomes more ironic—or maddening—when we take up the many massed sightings of UFO's by large numbers of witnesses at the same time:

——August 1965. A fleet of UFO's flew over eight states, from North Dakota down to Texas, passing over Omaha, Oklahoma City, and other metropolises. A million people saw them, by a conservative estimate. (USAF verdict—the pieces of a burst Skyhook balloon.)

——1964-65-66. At Wanaque Dam, New Jersey, periodic appearances of UFO's were observed by several thousands at the scene, as well as throughout three nearby counties with a population of two million. Estimated observers—300,000. (Air Force statement: "We never received any reports from Wanaque witnesses.")

————September 1954. Practically the whole populace of Rome, Italy, fascinatedly watched a half-cigar hanging and maneuvering a mile high in broad daylight, for an hour. Witnesses—1,500,000. (Air Force comment for all overseas reports: "We have no knowledge of foreign sightings.")

————January 1966. A UFO was seen by some 10,000 people in Perth, Australia, and was photographed in color.

Yet all of these multiple witnesses, in the eyes of the Air Force, saw nothing at all or were suffering from mass hallucination. It is bad enough when you see something that *isn't* there, but what would psychiatrists say of the USAF, which does not "see" something, via reliable evidence, that *is* there.

Life magazine perhaps summed it up best (January 6, 1958): "During the ensuing year there will be authenticated sightings of roughly 200 UFO's, of which the Pentagon will be able to disprove 210."

Another small but significant poll was taken by A3c John Prytz, USAF, while in uniform at his base (*Flying Saucers* magazine, Ray Palmer publication, October 1966). In answer to his question "Do you believe in UFO's?" 451 out of 548 enlisted airmen replied "yes." More impressively, 480 officers out of 590 were in the affirmative.

When asked if they thought there was "censorship" of the truth about UFO's by the Air Force, an overwhelming 507 out of 590 emphatically agreed.

They ought to know. It is Air Force pilots who, before the USAF clamped down in 1954, turned in the highest percentage (17.1%) of reports of any single group. The results of a poll taken among them should thus carry great weight.

Then, in his book *The Report on Unidentified Flying Objects,* Captain Edward J. Ruppelt stated that even back in 1950 "in a nationwide poll, it was found that only 6% of the country's 150,697,361 people agreed with the colonel and said, 'There aren't such things' (as flying saucers)."

But even if the USAF shrugs off the true totals, whether in the U.S. or elsewhere, of actual UFO sightings, what does it think of its own "hard core" list of 652 unknowns today, which were never explained away, not even by its expert staff of explainer-awayers?

Those 652 admitted unknowns hang like the sword of Damocles over the trembling ATIC of the USAF.

Unscientific Scientists

Second only to the Air Force for being remiss in investigating the UFO riddle properly is the scientific community.

Their public utterances at times have been utterly unenlightened and supremely arrogant. The following account is typical of how the hierarchs of entrenched science react to any and all flying saucer cases, even celebrated ones.

On "The Open Mind" program (WNBC-TV) in 1965 the panelists included John G. Fuller, author of two outstanding UFO documentary books (*Incident at Exeter* and *The Interrupted Journey*), and Dr. Donald H. Menzel, astronomer emeritus of Harvard University.

The comments of Dr. Menzel, who previously wrote a denigrating book on saucers (*The World of Flying Saucers,* coauthored by Lyle G. Boyd, Doubleday, New York City, 1963) are quite typical of the *nonscientific* approach of scientists in general to UFO's. Excerpts from the transcript follow:

FULLER: I went up to Exeter (New Hampshire) for 24 days. I interviewed 60 people. I tape-recorded 70 hours of testimony. I crossexamined these people. . . . I tried to disprove (their stories) . . . Now, were you up there in Exeter, Dr. Menzel, to investigate this?

MENZEL: No, I was not . . . because I don't have time to investigate every one of these cases.

(Later, referring to one of the key UFO witnesses at Exeter:)

MENZEL: It was certainly clear from the whole picture that the man was frightened—frightened to death and he became hysterical. . . .

FULLER: Which man?

MENZEL: The original man who saw the . . .

FULLER: What was his name?

MENZEL: I'm sorry, I don't know his name.

FULLER: How old was he?

MENZEL: (???)

Dr. Menzel didn't know and tried to change the subject. And it turned out, his whole knowledge of the Exeter sightings was very vague, based on erroneous newspaper accounts he had seen—which he accepted as "true," as no scientist ever should.

John Fuller kept pointing out that you can't judge people or what they saw from a distant ivory tower. You must go there and interview them, see the awed look in their eyes, hear the ring of sincerity in their voices, before you can autocratically denounce their sightings as "hysteria."

In my opinion scientists like Dr. Menzel are pursuing the very opposite of the true goal of science, which is to *investigate* new phenomena. And very thoroughly and exhaustively. Making lordly pronouncements and judgments without all the facts is a job for loose-tongued radio pundits and their ilk, hardly for scientists.

"Invisible College"

However, it must be quickly added that this is not an indictment of all scientists. A growing group has rolled up its sleeves and is pitching in, taking sides in this controversy—the side of the UFO's. Other eminent men could also be key witnesses for the defense, in a mythical trial, in the case of "Established authority versus the saucers."

Foremost among them would be Dr. J. Allen Hynek, who was the Air Force's Consultant on UFO's for 18 years, but who is now apparently steering his own course, as his recent words show (*Newsweek,* in the Periscope, May 1, 1967):

"There is an invisible college—an anonymous group of physicists, astronomers, and other scientists—who believe that UFO's are important to investigate and not just the product of incompetent investigation and hysteria. . . . If I could get $1 million, I could have 50 first-rate scientists working on the problem."

In the Soviet Union, Professor F. Zigel says: "The phenomena of the UFO's today should be considered global. . . . There can be no doubt that UFO's exist."

Frank Edwards, news commentator and author (*Flying Saucers—Serious Business,* Bantam Books, New York City, 1965) asked this question of a scientist: "Mr. Halstead, could the UFO's of our time be space ships?"

To which the late Frank Halstead, curator of Darling Observatory, Minnesota, replied: "Frankly, sir, they could hardly be anything else."

From South America comes this corroborating voice from Professor Gabriel Alvial, Carro Calan Observatory: "There is scientific evidence that strange objects are circling our planet. It is lamentable that governments have drawn a veil of secrecy around this matter."

To which Professor Claudio Anguila, director of the same observatory, adds a brief, classic comment: "We are not alone in the universe."

I am sure, to the layman who reads this book and has never been acquainted with UFO matters before, all this will come as a shocking surprise that many authoritative voices proclaim the existence of UFO's, whereas the Air Force and U.S. Government have foisted the fairy tale on Americans that it is all "nothing."

The United States is probably the furthest behind, of all major nations on earth, in comprehending the true picture of the saucer phenomenon. And the U.S. Government, supposedly the "leader" of the free world, has in this instance completely shirked leadership, probably to a detrimental degree. Once again we are leaving the door wide open for the Soviet Union to make the first dramatic announcement to the world—"We have established contact with the UFO's and held a conference with the saucerians from another world in outer space."

Has the USAF or government ever pondered this possible debacle? All the world would forever after condemn the U.S. for missing the greatest "beat" in history, though they had, through voluminous USAF files, the full evidence in front of them for at least a decade.

Pattern Proof

But rather than take the testimony of either UFO supporters or skeptics, pro or con, let us summarize what may be the most convincing evidence of all to everyone —namely, the *patterns* that are the keynote of this book. What do they prove, if anything?

Looking over the complete list in compact form will bring forth the full impact and import of the series of UFO patterns:

1) PATTERN OF SPECIFIC UFO SHAPES
—Discs, globes, ovoids, teardrops, and cylinders constitute 90% of all sightings (26% discs alone).

2) PATTERN OF MIRACULOUS MANEUVERS
—Fantastic speeds, acceleration, straight-up flight, right-angle turns, fleet formations, wild "sky dances."
—Ubiquitous rocking or "wobbling" motion when hovering.
—"Falling leaf" descent almost universal.

3) PATTERN OF COLOR CHANGES
—White for hovering, red or orange for acceleration, blue-white for hyper-speed, green for sharp turns (in general).
—Rotating lights and blinding searchlight beams on low-flying saucers.

4) PATTERN OF SILENT FLIGHT
—Fly noiselessly, unlike all earthly craft.
—At close range, low "whines" or hums heard, indicating some kind of noncombustion engine.

5) PATTERN OF ELECTROMAGNETIC EFFECTS
—Car engines stalled, radio and headlights blacked out.
—Electrical blackouts in cities, associated with passage of UFO's.
—"Ray burns" and "paralysis" experienced by humans.
—Animals greatly disturbed by "unseen forces."

6) PARANORMAL PATTERN
—Fear of the unknown during sightings.
—Instinctive feeling of "unearthliness."
—Weirdness of many UFO's.

7) PATTERN OF ANGEL HAIR

–Documented sightings of "fluff" falling.

–Unlike any material known on earth.

–Proven not to be spider webbing.

8) PATTERN OF SAUCER WAVES

–Waves also occurred in previous centuries.

–Foo-fighters and ghost-rockets in waves, prior to
rnold's 1947 sighting.

–"Mission waves" in succession of disc "scouts," cigar
other-ships, green fireball "missiles," EM effects,
rouped landings.

9) PATTERN OF UFONAUTS

–High percentage of "little men."

–Hairy dwarfs and various giants.

–UFOnaut landings mainly during night hours.

10) PATTERN OF INTELLIGENT CONTROL

–Subpatterns of UFOnaut curiosity, reactions to hu-
nans, precision UFO formations, piloted sky maneuvers.

11) PATTERN OF MIND-MADE MACHINES

–Powered flight indications.

–Structural details of UFO's.

–Silent, nonearthly propulsion system.

2) PATTERN OF UFO "MISSIONS"

–Mother ships releasing disc "scouts."

–Possible photographic, observation, and reconnaissance
nissions.

–Earth samples gathered by landing UFOnauts.

–Low-flying saucers that follow planes, cars, trains,
ships, and people.

13) PATTERN OF HOSTILITY (negative)

–Plane crashes, "kidnappings," green fireball "missiles"
presumed.

–Orthotenic survey of earth as if for conquest.

–But "pattern of peace" more likely.

14) PATTERN OF NONCONTACT POLICY

–"Shyness" of UFO's and UFOnauts.

–Silent secrecy of saucerians and why.

15) PATTERN OF UNEARTHLINESS

–UFO's "alien" in every way.

–Possible origins—ocean, future, hollow earth, radiant

space beings, dimension beings, interstellar visitors. /
"unearthly."

—"Fade" phenomena, cloud-cigars, vanishments mig
mean "interdimensional travel."

—Galactic "United Planets" organization.

16) USAF PARADOX PATTERN

—Air Force cover-up while secretly investigating.

—Possible secret contact, unannounced.

—Scientists remiss in not studying UFO's.

The UFO Verdict

Not all of these presumed patterns are valid, of cours
Some will prove false if contact is ever made with th
saucerians. But almost unshakable are certain pattern
that, by sheer weight of circumstantial evidence, testify t
the *reality* of the UFO's in our skies.

That is all this book attempts to do—once and for a
to take the UFO phenomenon out of the "myth" categor
and place it firmly in the "reality" category, despite al
the brush-off machinations of the Air Force, the govern
ment, and orthodox science.

The patterns that I feel most strongly support the reali
ty of UFO's as flying machines are:

Repeated UFO shapes in worldwide reports.

Fantastic Maneuvers, a common denominator in sight
ings.

Color changes almost universal.

EM effects cases piling up steadily.

UFOnaut little men numerously reported.

Saucer unearthliness in many eerie ways.

UFO waves indicating nonrandom intelligent planning

Structural details massively reported beyond further
doubt.

The flying saucers are here. The UFO's are real. The
only thing unreal is earth's attitude toward these signifi
cant objects and their mysterious masters, who may well
be here to tell us of a brotherhood of worlds in the uni
verse.

U.S. AIR FORCE TECHNICAL INFORMATION

This questionnaire has been prepared so that you can give the U.S. Air Force as much information as possible concerning the unidentified aerial phenomenon that you have observed. Please try to answer as many questions as you possibly can. The information that you give will be used for research purposes. Your name will not be used in connection with any statements, conclusions, or publications without your permission. We request this personal information so that if it is deemed necessary, we may contact you for further details.

---

1. When did you see the object?

_____ _____ _____
Day   Month   Year

2. Time of day: _____ _____
                 Hour   Minutes

(Circle One):   A.M.   or   P.M.

---

3. Time Zone:

(Circle One): a. Eastern
              b. Central
              c. Mountain
              d. Pacific
              e. Other _____

(Circle One): a. Daylight Saving
              b. Standard

---

4. Where were you when you saw the object?

_____

Nearest Postal Address   City or Town   State or County

---

5. How long was object in sight? (Total Duration) _____ _____ _____
                                                   Hours   Minutes Seconds

        a. Certain   c. Not very sure
        b. Fairly certain   d. Just a guess

5.1 How was time in sight determined? _____

5.2 Was object in sight continuously? Yes _____ No _____

---

6. What was the condition of the sky?

        DAY   NIGHT
        a. Bright   a. Bright
        b. Cloudy   b. Cloudy

---

7. IF you saw the object during DAYLIGHT, where was the SUN located as you looked at the object?

(Circle One): a. In front of you   d. To your left
              b. In back of you   e. Overhead
              c. To your right   f. Don't remember

FORM
FTD OCT 62 164   This form supersedes FTD 164, Jul 61, which is obsolete.

8. IF you saw the object at NIGHT, what did you notice concerning the STARS and MOON?

8.1 STARS (Circle One):

a. None
b. A few
c. Many
d. Don't remember

8.2 MOON (Circle One):

a. Bright moonlight
b. Dull moonlight
c. No moonlight – pitch dark
d. Don't remember

9. What were the weather conditions at the time you saw the object?

CLOUDS (Circle One):

a. Clear sky
b. Hazy
c. Scattered clouds
d. Thick or heavy clouds

WEATHER (Circle One):

a. Dry
b. Fog, mist, or light rain
c. Moderate or heavy rain
d. Snow
e. Don't remember

10. The object appeared: (Circle One):

a. Solid
b. Transparent
c. Vapor
d. As a light
e. Don't remember

11. If it appeared as a light, was it brighter than the brightest stars? (Circle One):

a. Brighter
b. Dimmer
c. About the same
d. Don't know

11.1 Compare brightness to some common object:

_____

12. The edges of the object were:

(Circle One): a. Fuzzy or blurred
b. Like a bright star
c. Sharply outlined
d. Don't remember

e. Other _____

_____

_____

13. Did the object:

(Circle One for each question)

a. Appear to stand still at any time?	Yes	No	Don't know
b. Suddenly speed up and rush away at any time?	Yes	No	Don't know
c. Break up into parts or explode?	Yes	No	Don't know
d. Give off smoke?	Yes	No	Don't know
e. Change brightness?	Yes	No	Don't know
f. Change shape?	Yes	No	Don't know
g. Flash or flicker?	Yes	No	Don't know
h. Disappear and reappear?	Yes	No	Don't know

14. Did the object disappear while you were watching it? If so, how?

15. Did the object move behind something at any time, particularly a cloud?

(Circle One):   Yes   No   Don't Know.   IF you answered YES, then tell what

it moved behind: _____

_____

16. Did the object move in front of something at any time, particularly a cloud?

(Circle One):   Yes   No   Don't Know.   IF you answered YES, then tell what

in front of: _____

17. Tell in a few words the following things about the object:

a. Sound _____

b. Color _____

18. We wish to know the angular size. Hold a match stick at arm's length in line with a known object and note how much of the object is covered by the head of the match. If you had performed this experiment at the time of the sighting, how much of the object would have been covered by the match head?

19. Draw a picture that will show the shape of the object or objects. Label and include in your sketch any details of the object that you saw such as wings, protrusions, etc., and especially exhaust trails or vapor trails. Place an arrow beside the drawing to show the direction the object was moving.

20. Do you think you can estimate the speed of the object?

(Circle One)   Yes   No

IF you answered YES, then what speed would you estimate? _____

21. Do you think you can estimate how far away from you the object was?

(Circle One)   Yes   No

IF you answered YES, then how far away would you say it was? _____

22. Where were you located when you saw the object? (Circle One):

a. Inside a building
b. In a car
c. Outdoors
d. In an airplane (type)
e. At sea
f. Other _____

23. Were you (Circle One)

a. In the business section of a city?
b. In the residential section of a city?
c. In open countryside?
d. Near an airfield?
e. Flying over a city?
f. Flying over open country?
g. Other _____

24. IF you were MOVING IN AN AUTOMOBILE or other vehicle at the time, then complete the following questions:

24.1 What direction were you moving? (Circle One)

a. North   c. East   e. South   g. West
b. Northeast   d. Southeast   f. Southwest   h. Northwest

24.2 How fast were you moving? _____ miles per hour.

24.3 Did you stop at any time while you were looking at the object?

(Circle One)   Yes   No

25. Did you observe the object through any of the following?

a. Eyeglasses   Yes   No   e. Binoculars   Yes   No
b. Sun glasses   Yes   No   f. Telescope   Yes   No
c. Windshield   Yes   No   g. Theodolite   Yes   No
d. Window glass   Yes   No   h. Other _____

26. In order that you can give as clear a picture as possible of what you saw, describe in your own words a common object or objects which, when placed up in the sky, would give the same appearance as the object which you saw.

27. In the following sketch, imagine that you are at the point shown. Place on "A" on the curved line to show how high the object was above the horizon (skyline) when you *first* saw it. Place a "B" on the same curved line to show how high the object was above the horizon (skyline) when you *last* saw it. Place an "A" on the compass when you *first* saw it. Place a "B" on the compass where you *last* saw the object.

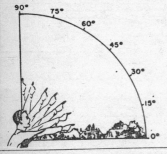

28. Draw a picture that will show the motion that the object or objects made. Place an "A" at the beginning of the path, a "B" at the end of the path, and show any changes in direction during the course.

29. IF there was MORE THAN ONE object, then how many were there? _____
    Draw a picture of how they were arranged, and put an arrow to show the direction that they were traveling.

30. Have you ever seen this, or a similar object before. If so give date or dates and location.

31. Was anyone else with you at the time you saw the object? (Circle One)   Yes   No

31.1 IF you answered YES, did they see the object too? (Circle One)   Yes   No

31.2 Please list their names and addresses:

32. Please give the following information about yourself:

NAME _____
          Last Name   First Name   Middle Name

ADDRESS _____
                    Street   City   Zone   State

TELEPHONE NUMBER _____ AGE _____ SEX _____

Indicate any additional information about yourself, including any special experience, which might be pertinent.

33. When and to whom did you report that you had seen the object?

_____   _____   _____
   Day   Month   Year

34. Date you completed this questionnaire: _____   _____   _____
                                                        Day   Month   Year

35. Information which you feel pertinent and which is not adequately covered in the specific points of the questionnaire or a narrative explanation of your sighting.

A Word to the Wise About Your Sighting

Conventional objects, seen under unusual lighting conditions or special circumstances, account for anywhere from 70% to 90% of most UFO sightings. Herewith is a list of the most common objects that can fool a person into thinking he has seen a flying saucer.

A—*High-altitude weather balloons.* Thousands of these are sent up each day over the U.S., and sometimes at extreme heights (above 50,000 feet) the glint of sunlight can give them the appearance of hovering or slow-moving discs, globes, ovoids, etc.

Clues to true identity

—Always slow-moving, never faster than the prevailing wind and in the *same direction* (at high altitudes).

—Do not dart up or down wildly.

—A check with the local weather station will reveal if a weather balloon was sent up in that area.

B—*Jets and aircraft.* High-flying jet planes and even low-altitude planes are often deceiving, especially if wind conditions mute their sounds. Sunlight or moonlight can be reflected so that the plane seems to have no wings, like a UFO.

Clues to true identity

—Almost always has some sound, even if subdued.

—Makes no right-angle turns or other "impossible" maneuvers in the sky.

—Takes long minutes to cross the sky and fade from sight, whereas most UFO's vanish in seconds.

C——*Astronomical Objects.* Bright planets, meteors, aurora effects, even brilliant fixed stars, often deceive the observer, especially when low over the horizon where the distorting effects of the thick atmosphere can make them do amazing "tricks." Also, any planet or bright star viewed from a *moving vehicle* will seem to "follow you," dipping behind hills and "speeding" ahead as you make a turn, etc. Venus in particular, which at certain seasons is the brightest object in the night sky next to the moon, is reported over and over as a "UFO" by excitable people.

Clues to true identity

—Venus (or any planet or star) does not move except very very slowly, as all the star-field does. No sudden motion—except if you are in a moving car, by an optical illusion—and no change of color or size (although special atmospheric conditions can cause color changes and apparent change in size).

—No actual form is ever seen, just the starlike source of light, which should call for caution immediately.

—A check of any current star chart for that season will show whether Venus (or Jupiter, Mars, etc.) could be in that position at the time "sighted." If not, it might be a UFO.

Meteors sometimes flash across the sky and remain in view long enough to make the viewer think it is a UFO, but the characteristics of meteors should leave little room for error—short duration of sighting (a few seconds at most); continuous, unswerving flight (though at times, due to perspective, they may seem to curve sharply and slant upward for a moment); no stopping and starting up again.

Fireballs are huge, blazing meteors that are flying more or less parallel to earth's surface and thus can stay in view longer, but they too are characterized by continuous and unvarying flight and a short visibility. If in doubt, check with your local weather bureau or planetarium before reporting a UFO.

D——*Earth satellites.* There are over 250 satellites in orbit today (1967-68), both Russian and American. Many of them are "secret" and no overflight data is given for them (such as the Air Force's reconnaissance satellites and the Soviet's Cosmos series of "spy vehicles"); hence you may see them startlingly soar over you any twilight or predawn period, some of them in such low orbits that they are far brighter than any star or even Venus (especially the giant Russian satellites weighing half a ton or more). Also, at the rate of 10 a month, old satellites "decay" in their orbit (fall lower) and suddenly reenter the atmosphere, burning up in a fiery display that may well look like a "UFO" to the observer.

Clues to true identity

—Satellites travel a very *steady* course through the field of stars.

—The brightest ones in nearby orbits (100 to 300 miles high) traverse from horizon to horizon in less than 15 minutes and never hover.

—During reentry burn-up, they plunge down quite like a blazing meteor, at a downward slanting curve, never changing course or halting.

—A check with the Satellite Tracking Center in Cambridge, Massachusetts, will quickly tell you if a satellite was scheduled to fall that night. The public is invited to phone (called "Dial-A-Satellite Service"). The number is 617-864-7910, Extension 364; for special information, 617-491-1497; Smithsonian in Washington, D.C. also gives the same data at 202-737-8855.

E——*Other objects:* flocks of birds, peculiar clouds, windblown debris, missiles, fireworks, chaff from jet planes (antiradar), etc. These are all self-evident, and any one taking the time to narrowly observe these objects will not be fooled. They will not have the key characteristics of UFO's, such as incredible flight acrobatics, or distinct shapes, or the change of colors that is usually associated with UFO's.

F——*Illusionary Sightings.* Be it admitted that the Air Force is right in saying some people report nonexistent phenomena, which include sky reflections of ground objects due to "inversions" (layers of cold air over hot air); mirages, but these are rare; searchlights moving over clouds; the contrails of jetplanes; and pure hallucinations.

Clues to true identity

—Optical illusions of any type will look "non-material," often semitransparent or "hazy."

—They will act in a "crazier" manner than UFO's ever did, changing shape and form and brightness with chaotic rapidity.

—A generous dose of common sense or shrewd analysis will convince the observer he is seeing something without substance of an illusionary nature, if he does not instantly rush to the phone to report his "amazing UFO."

G——*Hoaxes.* These, of course, are practiced everywhere at times, particularly by college students and youngsters. Often their devices are ingenious—like a flare or candle in a gas-inflated plastic bag—which behave erratically and can be mistaken for a UFO. There is not much defense the innocent victim has against these shoddy, immature tricks except to think over whether any local group of school kids or teenage pranksters could be the cause of the "sighting," then waiting for the police or newspaper reporters to dig up the culprits, which happens in the majority of such cases.

Rules to follow

—Never rush off half-cocked to phone in or write down your supposed "UFO."

—Observe carefully, noting all significant details.

—With a bit of common sense, you won't be one of the large majority of excitable people who look up and see a "UFO" no matter what pops up in the sky, when a moment's reflection and careful observation will reveal that it is nothing mysterious at all but merely an earthly object seen under special conditions. These people, who year in and year out report Venus, balloons, jets, bird flocks, and what-not for "flying saucers," are a detriment to the UFO cause. They cost the Air Force, and private UFO investigation groups such as NICAP, a large amount of wasted time. They are contributing nothing to the pursuit of knowledge or science. Each person looking up in the sky and

seeing what he thinks is a "mysterious object"
should, unless he is an irresponsible and mis-
guided idiot, make the necessary mental "tests"
and cautious observations to make sure he is not
calling an IFO (Identified Flying Object) a UFO.
He is the one who *does* deserve ridicule and scorn
for his worthless "sighting." *Only legitimate sightings of true UFO's can help solve the great riddle.*

The Following is a list of the proportions of all the
sightings mentioned above:

A— 2.5%
B—22.0%
C—24.0%
D—12.5%
E— 5.2%
F— 1.1%
G— 0.5%
    12.7%   (Listed as insufficient data by USAF)
    19.5%   (Listed as *"pending"* by *USAF*)
    ————
    100.0%

Dr. Jacques Vallee, author of two outstanding UFO
books (*Anatomy of a Phenomenon: UFO's* and *Challenge to
Science: The UFO Enigma*), has devised perhaps the most
scientific analysis of types of flying saucers, which should
be helpful to any UFO researcher. The listing follows:

Type I. . . . *Landers or low-flying UFO's*
    I-A—Low-flyers over the land
    I-B—Low-flyers over water
    I-C—Landers from which UFOnauts emerge
    I-D—UFO's that follow earth vehicles

Type II . . . *Cigars and mother ships*
    II-A—When in motion
    II-B—Stationary and smaller craft emerge
    II-C—Mother ship and small craft are separated
    when observed

Type III. . . . *Discs, spheroids, ovoids*
    III-A—In descending pattern of falling leaf
    III-B—Flies close, hovers, goes on
    III-C—Halts and changes color or manifests
    other phenomena (EM effects, etc.)

III-D—Dogfights betwees UFO's, or erratic solo flight

III-E—UFO changes course to cruise or circle, then departs at great speed

Type IV. . . . *All shapes of UFO's when in motion*

IV-A—In continuous flight

IV-B—Flight pattern changes near an airplane

IV-C—Formations, fleets, echelons

IV-D—Continuous flight in zigzags or undulations

Type V . . . *Fuzzy and "nonmaterial" UFO's*

V-A—Large globes or masses of "mist" or "foggy lights"

V-B—Starlike objects that dart around and alternately hang motionless

V-C—Rapid flight like meteors and fireballs but slower, sometimes with course changes

A pamphlet entitled *Project 'B' 1966* issued by John Keel, indefatigable UFO investigator, lists the following intriguing data about the 1,060 sightings in 1966, the second highest year (after 1952) in the Air Force's records:

—More than 10,000 reports came in from all over the world.

—A high percentage of 7.3% were Type I (low-flying and landing UFO's), more than any other year.

—An oddity is the fact that 20% of all sightings occurred on Wednesdays, 17% on Thursdays, while Tuesdays were lowest with 7%

—1966 repeated a strange pattern that started in 1964 and continued in 1965, and also occurred in 1967—the largest number of sightings in each of those years (1964 through 1967) were reported in the 4th week of March, the 4th week of July, the 3rd week in August, and the 3rd week in September. What the significance of this could be, nobody knows.

—The largest "flap" during the 1966 waves took place on the single night of August 16th, between the hours of 9:00 P.M. and 11:00 P.M. The most sightings that night came from Minnesota, Wisconsin, Arkansas, South Dakota, and New Jersey.

—Throughout 1966 the largest number of sightings came from (in order) Ohio, Nebraska, Oregon, California, and Minnesota. But UFO reports came from all 50 states.

—Most sightings occurred in isolated, thinly populated sections of the country. Kentucky and West Virginia have had almost continuous sightings since the summer of 1966, well into 1967.

—If the flying saucers were purely a psychological phenomenon, sightings would have increased in heavily populated areas, especially in large cities with the highest incidence of disturbed people. But the areas of the most dense population account for the least number of reports, obviously eliminating any subjective/psychological/illusionary basis for UFO's.

—If the UFO's were natural phenomena, such as meteors or flaming bolides, which travel at tremendous speed (average 60 miles per second), reports on any given date or time would have to come from several states over which the bright meteor was seen, and at almost the *same time*. Saucer reports belie this entirely, often being single sightings seen by only one person or one small town. When what seems to be the the same UFO is reported along a string of towns, the time differences are so great, in total, that no meteor could move that slowly (nor can it stop, start, change course, and perform aerial tricks like reported UFO's).

Mr. Keel makes the following general observations:

—There is no slightest evidence that the UFO's are extraterrestrial vehicles from outer space. All "hardware" specimens allegedly coming from UFO's have been analyzed as ordinary earthly materials.

—Since 1896 there have been 2,500 recorded cases in which witness claimed to see UFOnauts, 92% of which were called "humanoid" or humanlike in form, with differences in size only at times (such as the "little men" and sometimes people 6 or 7 feet tall).

—Oddly, the UFOnauts seem to come down over the same areas most frequently, year after year, with Ohio in the lead.

—There are now hundreds of cases—mostly reported by reliable people such as police officers and pilots—in which the UFO's responded to or returned light signals flashed by the witnesses.

—The overwhelming mass of reports clearly indicates intelligent control of the UFO's and leaves little doubt that they are manned.

—If they are, by chance, the vehicles of some unknown earthly race (underground, seabottom, Antarctica, etc.) they are carrying on "a blatant violation of our air space, as well as an open violation of all our licensing and aircraft zoning laws," as Mr. Keel puts it.

In an additional write-up called *North America 1966, Development of a Great Wave,* John Keel points up many other fascinating facts relating to the inexplicable UFO's:

—Many times, after his first sighting, a witness was described by friends or relatives as a "changed person."

—Much of the press has begun to concentrate on the sightings made by sheriffs and other law officers. In March of 1966 alone, some 50 police officials made reports.

—The low-level and landing UFO's have increased sharply in 1966, more than double the former percentages.

—A number of people, after staring at the incredibly brilliant UFO's had red and swollen eyes, even hours or days later.

—A rash of sightings told of UFO's pursuing individual people or families, often right up to the door of their homes, apparently to observe them closely.

Mr. Keel continues with a breakdown of the 1966 "flap":

—*Geographically,* many sightings followed a pattern along rivers and interstate highways.

—*Technically* there was the usual pattern of concentrated sightings at Air Force bases, arsenals, military installations, chemical factories, power plants, dams, transformer stations, and radio-TV broadcasting antennas.

—*Monitoring* activity included many cases of UFO's pursuing cars, planes, and people on foot, as well as hovering over homes.

—*Reservoir sightings* continued on a large scale throughout the U.S.

—*Landing and direct contact* (seeing UFOnauts emerge) reports were higher in 1966 than any time before in the U.S.

John Keel finds that "altogether, these thousands of reports mount up to an alarming picture. Perhaps they indicate that the UFO's are now engaged in a massive final stage of operations."

He adds that "my repeated visits to the Pentagon have convinced me that the U.S. Air Force is not genuinely interested in this problem. They have made no real attempt to interfere with the UFO activity in the flap areas, and they have shown no real interest in the complaints from citizens living in those areas."

In conclusion, Keel states: "The intensive UFO activity seems to support APRO's theory (Aerial Phenomena Research Organization, Arizona) that our population is now being rapidly prepared to accept their existence and deal emotionally with the fantastic social changes which their arrival is sure to foster."